Perrin

U.S. Navy Fighter Squadrons in World War II

By
Barrett Tillman

Specialty Press

ISBN: 0-933424-74-4

Library of Congress Catalog Card No.: 97-66086

Text by Barrett Tillman

Published by:
Specialty Press Publishers and Wholesalers
11481 Kost Dam Road
North Branch, MN 55056
Phone: 800-895-4585

Book Trade Distribution by:
Voyageur Press
123 North Second Street
Stillwater, MN 55082
Phone: 800-888-9653
Fax: 612-430-2211

Printed in the United States of America

TABLE OF CONTENTS

PREFACE

United States Navy aces—and fighter pilots generally—have been an important part of my personal, professional, and aviation life. Aside from the contributions they have made to many of my previous books, tailhook aviators have been warm in their acceptance and generous with their encouragement. I've grown especially close to the aerial hunters of the VF-9 Hellcats, VF-11 Sundowners, and VF-19 Satan's Kittens.

Among the aviators who contributed directly to this volume are O.C. "Buck" Bailey of VF-28 and and Bruce Weber of VF-34, plus the late Malcolm "Mac" Wordell, formerly CAG-44. Documentation and other assistance came unstintingly from Bill Hess, Frank Olynyk, and Jim Sawruk, with archival support from Roy Grossnick of the Naval Aviation History Office and Hill Goodspeed of the Naval Aviation Museum library.

In researching this volume, I recall some spirited "discussions" about all manner of esoterica, ranging from the Meaning of Life on up: such arcane facts as the number of turns to raise the F4F's hand-cranked landing gear (28, plus one more to lock) or the original wood in most Essex-class ships' flight decks (Douglas Fir or Oregon Pine; most of the world's teak was controlled by Japan after 1940.)

Let there be no doubt: he who disputes with the aces had better be trimmed up and cruising on the step. And he who establishes himself as arbiter of aerial combat results treads in the rarified atmosphere where sane angels fear to flutter their wings. Nor is the situation much improved in striving to determine what the official record may be. Ships are sunk, records are lost, contradictions exist; it does not make for a cheerful enterprise.

However, after a half-dozen previous volumes of naval fighter history, I became increasingly concerned with the lack of any single book devoted to U.S. Navy fighter units and aces in WW II. After all, the Japanese Imperial Navy has been authoritatively detailed in that regard, and it was the loser! Furthermore, as this is written, we are a half-century gone from VJ-Day, and aces are dropping off the scope at the steady clip of two or three a month. Ultimately, it became a matter or now or never.

And if that isn't enough waffling and downright evasive maneuvering, I don't know what is. Besides, I can feel the onset of "pipper burn" as some veteran fighter pilot's mental/emotional gunsight begins tracking me after a real or perceived lapse.

As my dad used to shout at me during more than 500 hours of flying together, "Don't just sit there, Cadet. Do something!"

Mixture rich, full throttle and RPM. Gunsight's up, select Master Arm, turn into the threat, and fight's on...

Barrett Tillman
Honorary Sundowner
Honorary Fighter Ace

VF 101

INTRODUCTION TO FITRONS

During World War II, U.S. Navy fighter squadrons claimed nearly a fifteen-to-one victory-loss ratio over the Axis powers in aerial combat. Allowing for the historic average error, the actual difference was probably between nine and ten to one, but the essential fact remained unchanged: carrier- and land-based Wildcats, Hellcats, and Corsairs won the Pacific air war and contributed to victory in Europe and the Mediterranean.

The following squadron sketches generally follow a consistent format, but Navy fighting squadrons (FitRons in contemporary parlance) were subject to the same administrative whims and operational hiccups as other units of the era.

A quick word about designations. In the 1920s the Navy established generic letters for aviation squadrons: V for heavier than air and Z for lighter than air. Thus, fighters became VF.

Among those squadrons existing prior to 7 December 1941, the "geneology" is explained in simplified terms. Each chronology indicates when the unit was established (ships and air stations are commissioned; squadrons and air groups are established) and the year of redesignations. In nearly every case, the date 1937 refers to the Navy-wide reorganization of 1 July, when air groups were assigned to individual carriers and squadron numbers were brought in line with the ship's hull number. Thus, USS *Lexington* (CV-2) flew Fighting, Bombing, Scouting, and Torpedo Squadron Two. But those units belonged to Lexington Air Group, not Air Group Two. Numbered air groups did not appear until 1942, when events in the Pacific made a hash of the logical, orderly, pre-war system.

Relatively few FitRons survived 1945, but for those that did, short notes are included on their later careers. All carrier squadrons were redesignated 15 November 1946 and again about 1 September 1948, so a typical entry for VF-19 shows: redesignated VF-19A (1946) and VF-191 (1948.) To repeat the same dates would be redundant and use up more trees and ink.

There was a great deal of duplication during the war years, with about 160 squadron numbers among VF, VF(N), VBF, and VOF units. For instance, there were two VF-52s and a VF(N)-52 at various times. At least ten sets of fighter squadron numbers were duplicated during the war, sometimes without any obvious reason. One famous example is the July 1943 swap of VF-3 and VF-6, both honored units of long standing. In the end, the Shooting Star squadron became Felix the Cat and and the original Felix squadron became—Felix the Cat. Go figure.

Many WW II aviators will seek their squadrons in vain in these pages. However, of some 150 FitRons established during the war, at least 60 never got to combat. As a more or less arbitrary guideline, I have only detailed those fighter units known flying offensive missions in any theater before 15 August 1945.

When two squadrons deployed to combat bearing the same number, I have listed them separately, as in VF-18 (I) and VF-18 (II). In a handful of instances the same squadron with the same personnel and same identity changed numbers. (VF-41/VF-4 and VGF-11/VF-21, for example.) Therefore, I have entries for both numeral designations but have described the unit's wartime career under the most prominent designation, with appropriate notes for the other.

Some escort and light-carrier squadrons had two or more designations, usually with the same number. VGF-26, later VF-26, is such a case, and in these instances there is one entry only.

Combat losses are listed where available, but some of this data is surprisingly difficult to obtain. Under each squadron's heading of "combat record" are notations such as, "Lost 8 officers, 2 enlisted." This usually refers to those killed in action, but generally excludes prisoners of war.

My roster of Navy aces lists 371, which is fewer than the number recognized by my friends of the American Fighter Aces Association (AFAA). I have largely accepted the seminal work of Dr. Frank Olynyk as the bible in this regard, but have waffled somewhat by including a separate list of those who logically could be aces owing to lost records (Air Force bases never sink), uncertain definitions (as in the vague credit "assist"), and other vagaries of 50-plus years.

Each squadron entry indicates the number of aces produced by that unit. The specific number refers to those pilots credited with five or more aerial victories while in the squadron. Thus, Lt(jg) Youthly Puresome, Sr., might have scored one victory in VF(N)-48 and four in VF-54, and is a Navy ace but not an ace of either squadron.

The top scorer in some squadrons is listed thusly: Lt. Roger Ball, 8 (10). The first number represents the pilot's score in that squadron; the number in parentheses being his wartime total.

Because of the recent comprehensive works by Olynyk and AFAA, this volume contains few biographies. A thorough appendix is listed for readers wishing to examine individual aces in detail.

Additionally, there is the ticklish matter of 80-some composite squadrons. The VC outfits, indiginous to CVEs, did a fabulous job in every theater of action, flying off tiny carriers in all kinds of weather. On average, half of their planes were fighters, and they shot down more than 400 enemy aircraft while producing a half-dozen aces. We have listed all the CVE aces, whether they flew in VC or VF squadrons. I say "we" because it was a joint decision shared by my fine publisher, Jack Lambert of Phalanx. My phone is unlisted, but he's in the St. Paul directory, so please call him to lodge your complaints.

Finally, both Jack and I would welcome additions or corrections to these entries. Victory credits, "permanent" commanding officers (not acting COs) and dates of assuming command are especially solicited, as the official records often omit such material.

Besides, if we don't set it down, who will?

Hellcats of VF and VBF-17 prepare to launch a strike from *Hornet* CV-12 in March 1945.

Moral of the Work:

"Only fighter aircraft can keep our carriers afloat."
Lieutenant Commander John S. Thach
1942

Dedicated to three special friends:

Charlie Stimpson (1919-1983), fellow Sundowner
Butch Davenport (1918-1989), fellow elk hunter
Tom Blackburn (1912-1994), fellow author

I still miss you guys

VF-1 High Hatters

Chronology: established as VF-4 (1 May 43)
redesignated VF-1 (15 Jul 43)

Deployments:			
	Dets aboard CVEs	Nov 43	F6F-3
	Tarawa Atoll	Nov 43-Jan 44	F6F-3
	Yorktown (CV-10)	May-Aug 44	F6F-3
	Bennington (CV-20)	Jun-Sep 45	F6F-5, -5N, -5P

Combat record:101 victories, 3 aces. Lost 13 on deployments.
Top score: Lt. Richard T. Eastmond, 9.

Upon redesignation from VF-4 at Alameda, the new Fighting One re-established the previous VF-1's traditional High Hat identity. Reportedly the name originated with *Yorktown's* task group commander, Rear Adm. Jerry Bogan, who had flown with VF-1B (?) as a junior aviator in the 1930s.

"Smoke" Strean's squadron was separated from its parent air group in late 1943, providing detachments aboard escort carriers before flying from newly-won Tarawa Atoll in the Gilberts. Lt(jg) R.T. Eastmond, eventually the High Hatters' top ace, scored the first victory while flying from Tarawa on 22 December 1943.

Reunited with Air Group One in *Yorktown*, Strean's unit claimed 99 victories during the Marianas and Bonins operations of June and July 1944. Of these, 37 occurred during the "Turkey Shoot" of 19 June. The High Hatters also participated in the attack on the Japanese Mobile Fleet the next day.

A division of Fighting One F6F-3s returning to *Yorktown* (CV-10) during the summer battles of 1944. Cdr. "Smoke" Strean's squadron participated in the Marianas Turkey Shoot and was heavily involved in a series of strikes against Iwo Jima in June and July.

After reforming in October 1944, VF-1 deployed in *Bennington* during the summer of 1945. Led by former NAP Boogie Hoffman, Fighting One's opportunities for aerial combat were rare by then, and the only claim of the deployment was a Judy shot down on 13 August 1945—two days before cessation of hostilities.

Wartime COs:	Lt.Cdr. Bernard M. Strean	1 May 43
	Lt.Cdr. David C. Richardson	23 Oct 44
	Lt.Cdr. Melvin C. Hoffman	15 Dec 44

Disestablished: 25 Oct 45

VBF-1

Established: 2 Jan 45

Deployment: *Bennington* (CV-20) Jun-Sep 45, F4U-1D, FG-1D

Combat record: 3 victories. Lost 4 pilots on deployment.
Top score: Cdr. H.B. Harden and Lt(jg) R.M. Applegate, 1 each.

Commander, Naval Air Forces Pacific Fleet (ComAirPac) authorized establishment of the first 18 bombing-fighting (VBF) squadrons in January 1945. The action was intended to reduce the administrative workload of the 73-plane FitRons, which had grown to as many as 110 pilots. Usually the executive officer of the air group's fighter squadron assumed command of the VBF unit, with division organization remaining relatively intact.

VBF-1 was equipped with Corsairs, as were the majority of fighter-bomber squadrons established before deploying to combat. Though shipboard maintenance was somewhat complicated, tactical flexibility was enhanced by the F4U's versatility and speed.

Though VBF-1 scored only three confirmed kills (the first by CAG-1 H.B. Harden), the Corsairs developed more chances than VF-1's Hellcats. Two Japanese fighters (Franks and/or Jacks) were destroyed and another probably splashed over Bungo Strait on 24 July, followed by a Judy dive-bomber on 9 August. Four pilots contributed to these victories.

Wartime COs: Lt.Cdr. Robert P. Ross 2 Jan 45

Disestablished: 25 Oct 45

VOF-1

Established: 15 Dec 43

Deployment: *Tulagi* (CVE-72) Aug 44 F6F-5

Combat record: 6 victories. Lost 2 pilots on deployment.
Top score: Ens. E.W. Olszewski, 2

Observation-Fighting Squadron One was trained in spotting naval gunfire in support of amphibious operations. Originally equipped with F4U-1s, the unit successfully carrier-qualified in Corsairs before being told the Voughts were "unsafe." Thus, VOF-1 received Hellcats in March 1944 before embarking for Operation Anvil-Dragoon, the invasion of Southern France in August.

Beginning 15 August, VOF-1 flew scores of recon and strike sorties, interdicting German transportation and calling gunfire support for U.S. Army troops. Only eight Luftwaffe aircraft were shot down during the two-week operation, six credited to VOF-1 and two to VF-74 Hellcats. Lt.Cdr. Bush Bringle's squadron lost five planes during 13 days on the line, but Ens. Ed Olszewski emerged as top scorer of the short campaign, with two Junkers 52 transports shot down on 21 August.

Wartime CO: Lt.Cdr. William F. Bringle 15 Dec 43

Subsequent Record: Redesignated VOC-1 (18 Dec 44), re-equipped with FM-2s. Flew from *Marcus Island* and *Wake Island* in the Pacific, adding 20 aerial victories against Japan.

Disestablished 17 Sep 45.

VOF-1 F6F-5 from escort carrier *Tulagi* launches from H.M.S. *Emperor* during the invasion of southern France in August 1944. Originally established with F4Us, Observation Fighting Squadron One converted to Hellcats for Anvil-Dragoon, then reformed as VOC-1 flying FM-2 Wildcats in the Pacific. Lt.Cdr. "Bush" Bringle's globetrotting squadron specialized in directing naval gunfire but shot down more than 20 Axis aircraft as well.

VF-2 (I) Flying Chiefs

Chronology: Established as VF-2B (Jul 1927)
Redesignated VF-2S (1932), VF-2B (1933), VF-2 (1937)

Deployments: *Lexington* (CV-2) Dec 41-May 42 F2A-3, F4F-3

Combat record: 17 victories. Lost 7 officers, 2 enlisted.
Top score: Lt.Cdr. Ramsey, Lt(jg) P.G. Baker, Ens. E.R. Sellstrom, 3 each.

The Flying Chiefs were almost universally regarded as "the hottest outfit afloat" for most of their existence. Composed largely of noncommissioned aviators (Naval Aviation Pilots), Fighting Two boasted an extremely high order of skill and experience.

At the time of Pearl Harbor VF-2 flew Brewster Buffalos, and only acquired F4F Wildcats the following spring. The F2As, though relatively fast, proved unsuitable for sustained carrier operations owing to uacceptably weak landing gear.

The squadron's only combat occurred during the two-day Battle of the Coral Sea, the world's first engagement between aircraft carriers. On 7 May the CO, LtCdr Paul Ramsey, led the escort to *Lexington's* strike against the Japanese light carrier *Shoho.* "Ramsey's Lambsies" claimed six confirmed victories and three probables during the mission, including two by Ramsey himself and three by Lt(jg) Paul Baker, a former NAP.

Next day, the 8th, the enemy carriers *Shokaku* and *Zuikaku* exchanged air strikes with the U.S. force. Lt. Noel Gayler's division lost three planes and pilots on strike escort. In defending *Lexington* and *Yorktown*, VF-2 lost another pair of fighters, and while the squadron claimed 11 kills during the day, "Lady Lex" succumbed to torpedo damage.

The Flying Chiefs were disestablished in July, but their legacy lived on. Several of Ramsey's pilots became aces in other squadrons, including future COs Noel Gayler, Bill Eder, and Scoop Vorse.

Wartime CO: Lt.Cdr. Paul H. Ramsey Jul 41

Disestablished: 1 Jul 42

VF-2 (II) Rippers/Tall Dogs

Established: 1 Jun 43

Deployments:			
	Enterprise (CV-6)	Nov 43-Jan 44	F6F-3
	Hornet (CV-12)	Mar-Sep 44	F6F-3, -5, -5P

Combat record: 245 victories, 27 aces. Lost 7 on deployments.
Top score: Cdr. Dean, 11

The second Fighting Two was part of a numbered air group, unlike the Flying Chiefs who belonged to Lexington Air Group. Therefore, the Rippers became the first WW II fighting squadron to bear the same designation as a previous unit in the war. They also deployed with several combat-experienced pilots from VF-6 and 10.

Somewhat like VF-1, Cdr. Bill Dean's VF-2 spent months detached from its air group. From November 1943 to January 1944, FitRon Two relieved VF-6 in *Enterprise*, where CAG Butch O'Hare organized "bat teams" of one TBF and two F6Fs for night interceptions. O'Hare was killed on such a mission near the Gilberts in late November, flying with VF-2's Ens. Andy Skon. By early December Dean's pilots claimed five shootdowns.

Rejoining CAG-2 aboard the second *Hornet*, the Rippers began hunting ever-greater opportunities to engage airborne targets. Limited combat occurred in late March, but in June Dean's troops started producing aces in prodigious numbers. Pre-invasion strikes in the Marianas resulted in 26 victories on 11 June alone. During the fleet engagement of the 19th, the Rippers were credited with 43 victories, including six by a former enlisted pilot, Ens. Spider Webb. Four more came during the dusk attack on the Japanese fleet the following evening.

Cdr. William A. Dean, CO and leading ace of VF-2.

Next came two spectacular missions in the Bonins. During combats over and around Iwo Jima on 24 June, the Rippers claimed 62 confirmed victories, nearly matching VF-15's recent record of 68.5 during the Turkey Shoot. Another 30 claims occurred in the same area on 3 July.

Constantly given false end-of-cruise notice, the Rippers finally closed their victory log when Spider Webb downed a Tony over Manila on 22 September. By then Dean and 26 of his pilots had achieved acedom.

Upon reorganization, a new batch of VF-2 pilots unaccountably changed the well-known Ripper identity to the Tall Dogs, complete with logo of a giant Dalmatian astride a Japanese shrine. The war ended before the squadron or air group could redeploy.

Wartime COs:	Cdr. William A. Dean	1 Jun 43
	Cdr. Alfred I. Boyd, Jr.	28 Dec 44

Disestablished: 9 Nov 45

VF-3 (I)

Chronology: Established as VF-3 (23 Sep 1921)
Redesignated VF-2 (1922), VF-6 (1927), VF-6B (1927), VB-2B (1928), VF-6B (1930), VF-3 (1937)

Deployments:	*Saratoga* (CV-2)	Dec 41-Jan 42	F4F-3, -3A
	Lexington (CV-3)	Feb-Mar 42	F4F-3
	Yorktown (CV-5)	Jun 42	F4F-4
	Enterprise (CV-6)	1943	F4F-4
	Guadalcanal		F4F-4

Combat record: 52.5 victories, 2 aces. Lost 6 on deployment.
Top score: Lt.Cdr. John S. Thach, 6.

One of the most successful Navy fighter squadrons of the early war period, VF-3 boasted the Felix the Cat emblem from 1928. Under "Jimmy" Thach, Fighting Three enjoyed a reputation for gunnery and innovative tactics which was only enhanced by Lt(jg) Butch O'Hare's Medal of Honor action.

VF-3 parted company with *Saratoga* when she was torpedoed off Hawaii on 11 January 1942. Relieving VF-2 in *Lexington*, the Felix squadron repelled the first major air attack ever made upon a U.S. carrier. Nearing Rabaul, New Britain, on 20 February, Lex was beset by Betty bombers and Thach's pilots claimed 18 in two combats, losing one pilot. O'Hare's single-handed defense of the ship gained him a spot promotion to lieutenant commander and eventual command of the squadron.

One of the most famous naval aviation photos of WW II shows Lt.Cdr. Jimmy Thach and Lt(jg) Butch O'Hare flying their assigned Fighting Three Wildcats (F-1 and F-13) over Hawaiian waters in March 1942. The previous month VF-3 defended *Lexington* (CV-2) from land-based enemy bombers, claiming 18 destroyed. O'Hare was credited with five, making him the first Navy ace of the war. (credit Tailhook Assn.)

Thach led a VF-3 contingent aboard *Yorktown* for the Midway battle, augmenting the resident VF-42. In that climactic event, 4 June, VF-3 claimed more victories than the other two FitRons combined. One of the VF-42 veterans, Lt(jg) Scott McCuskey, splashed five raiders in two missions to become the Navy's second ace in a day.

With 52.5 victories in three days of combat from February to June, Fighting Three was the Navy's top-scoring FitRon. No further combat occurred for the first Felix squadron, though top-notch leadership succeeded Thach for the rest of the squadron's incarnation as Fighting Three.

For further details, see VF-6 (II).

Wartime Cos:		
Wartime Cos:	Lt.Cdr. John S. Thach	Dec 40
	Lt.Cdr. Edward H. O'Hare	19 Jun 42
	Lt. Louis H. Bauer	15 Jul 43)

Subsequent record: redesignated VF-6 (15 Jul 43)
Disestablished 29 Oct 45. See VF-6 (II).

VF-3 (II)

Chronology: established as VF-1B (1 Jul 1935)
redesignated VF-8B (1937), VF-6 (1937), VF-3 (15 Jul 43)

Deployments:		
	Guadalcanal/Solomons Jul-Sep 43	F4F-4
	Yorktown (CV-10) Oct 44-Mar 45	F6F-5, -5N, -5P

Combat record: 55 victories, one ace. Lost 17 on deployment.
Top score: Lt. John L. Schell, 5.

A source of the perennial confusion in Naval Aviation is the "Felix flop" designation exchanges of VF-3 and -6 in July 1943. At that time CO Lou Bauer considered replacing Fighting Six's 1935 Shooting Star emblem with VF-3's traditional Felix, but the squadron shortly returned to the U.S. to reform.

After shakeout of new aircraft and personnel, Fighting Three joined *Yorktown* in time for the Philippine campaign. The first victories were logged in mid-November, but the new year brought much greater opportunity. "Lambo" Lamberson's pilots claimed 15 victories over French Indochina 12 January 1945, then added 18 more during the initial two-day sweep of the Tokyo area in mid-February. Upon return to Honshu eight days later the Felix Hellcats downed nine more bandits to conclude their victory log for the war.

During the 1944-45 deployment, 39 pilots contributed to 55 victories. Lt.Cdr. Lamberson was killed over Okinawa on 22 January, with Ed Bayers succeeding him. The sole ace was Lt. John Schell, though Lt(jg) Jim Jones, with two kills in VF-3, added five more with VBF-3.

Wartime COs:		
	Lt. Louis H. Bauer	15 Jul 43
	Cdr. Frederick R. Schrader	1 Oct 43
	Lt.Cdr. William L. Lamberson	29 Aug 44
	Lt.Cdr. Edward H. Bayers	22 Jan 45

Subsequent record: Redesignated VF-3A (1946), VF-31 (1948) and still active in 1995 as the Tomcatters, flying F-14s.

Lt. (j.g.) Henry M. Rowland, VF-3, shows the battle damage his Hellcat sustained over Tokyo on 17 Feb 45. Rowland dished out more than he got, downing one Japanese fighter.

VBF-3

Established: 1 Feb 45

Deployments: *Yorktown* (CV-10) Feb-Mar 45 F6F-5

Combat record: 36 victories, one ace. No combat losses.
Top score: Lt(jg) J.M. Jones, 5 (7).

In its brief combat career, VBF-3 found airborne enemy aircraft on three days and shot down 36. It was one of the better performances among fighter-bomber squadrons.

When VF-3 split to form a VBF unit, Lt.Cdr. Fritz Wolf was already a combat-experienced fighter pilot. A prewar naval aviator, he joined the American Volunteer Group under Claire Chennault and was credited with four victories in the China-Burma theater. Returning to the Navy, he had to wait two and a half years for another shot at Japanese aircraft.

Despite poor weather, the two-day Tokyo strike in February 1945 presented VBF-3 with excellent opportunities. On the first day, the 16th, the Hellcats claimed 23 victories over Konoike and Kiaumigara Airfield. Next day another 13 airborne bandits were claimed, primarily near Utsononyia Airfield. In these two days, Lt(jg) John M. Jones (who had two previous victories with VF-3) became VBF-3's only ace by downing five fighters. He also logged the squadron's last claim, a probable during the return strikes to Tokyo on 25 February.

Fritz Wolf became an American fighter ace, however, downing a Tony on the 16th. Combined with his AVG score, it was his fifth victory of the war.

Wartime COs: Lt.Cdr. Fritz E. Wolf 2 Jan 45
Lt.Cdr. E.S. Gwathmey 19 May 45

Subsequent record: Redesignated VF-4A (1946) and VF-32 (1948). Still active in 1995, flying F-14s.

VF-4 (VF-41) Red Rippers

Chronology: established as VF-5 (Feb 1927)
redesignated VF-5S (1927), VF-5B (1928), VF-1B (1928), VF-5B (1930), VF-4 (1937), VF-41 (15 Mar 1941), VF-4 (5 Aug 43).

WW II deployments:			
	Ranger (CV-4)	Oct 42-Oct 43	F4F-4
	Bunker Hill (CV-17)	Nov 44	F6F-5
	Essex (CV-9)	Nov 44-Mar 45	F6F-5, -5P

Combat record: 76 victories, 2 aces. Losses unknown.
Top score: Lt. Will "W" Taylor, 6

As the first F4F squadron, Fighting 44 introduced the Wildcat to fleet service in late 1940. Then, embarked in *Ranger* for Operation Torch, the invasion of French Morocco, Lt.Cdr. Tommy Booth's VF-41 pilots claimed 14 Vichy planes shot down.

Still in *Ranger* a year later, the Red Rippers (now VF-4) supported a strike against German-controlled shipping in Bodo, Norway, 15 October 1943. The CAP splashed two snoopers, both shared by Lt(jg) Dean Laird with other pilots in the division.

VF-4 reformed with F6Fs and sailed to the Pacific in late 1944, briefly flying from *Bunker Hill* that November. Three Oscars were damaged over Leyte Gulf on Armistice Day, but seven confirmed came near Clark Field on the 13th—adding "meatballs" to the squadron's previous Vichy French and German kills.

Upon transfer to *Essex* on the 18th, Fighting Four encountered more frequent opposition. Philippine overland missions and CAPs on the 25th accounted for another 14 victories. On 14 December Lt.Cdr. Hammond became VF-4's first pilot with two Japanese kills, but was lost shortly thereafter, being succeeded by Lt. Lykes Boykin. The Rippers' best day of the war was 16 February 1945, when 16 kills were credited during the Tokyo strikes. Seven more were recorded the next day. Five more kills were logged by month's end, thus ending the Rippers' long war.

The Pacific cruise had added 60 victories to the record, and Lt. "Diz" Laird became the only Navy ace with confirmed kills against both Germany and Japan. Additionally, the Rippers probably were the only Navy squadron to shoot down aircraft of three Axis powers.

Wartime COs:	Lt.Cdr. Charles T. Booth	Mar 41
	Lt.Cdr. Malcolm T. Wordell	9 Dec 42
	Lt.Cdr. Charles L. Moore	21 Apr 43
	Lt.Cdr. Keene G. Hammond +	14 Mar 44
	Lt. Lykes M. Boykin	6 Jan 45
	Lt.Cdr. John E. Lacouture	18 May 45

Subsequent record: redesignated VF-1A (1946), VF-11 (1948). Disestablished 1959.

VF-5 (I)

Chronology: established as VF-3S (17 Aug 27)
redesignated VF-5B (??), VF-5 (1937)

Deployments:	*Saratoga* (CV-3)	Aug 42	F4F-4
	Guadalcanal	Sep-Oct 42	F4F-4

Combat record: 78 victories, 4 aces. Lost 12 officers, 5 enlisted.
Top score: Lt. Hayden M. Jensen, 7.

The original WW II Fighting Five was *Yorktown*'s (CV-5) F3F squadron which transitioned to F4Fs in 1941. Conducting Neutrality Patrol at the time of Pearl Harbor, VF-5 reached combat aboard *Saratoga* at the start of the Guadalcanal campaign. Disestablished in early 1943, the CV-5 squadron was succeeded by a subsequent unit which flew Hellcats and Corsairs. (Photo to come)

Fighting Five was a prewar member of Yorktown Air Group, but never flew combat from CV-5. At the time of Pearl Harbor, VF-5 was engaged in President Roosevelt's "neutrality patrol" and had no time to rejoin *Yorktown* before she sailed with *Ranger's* VF-42.

By the time Roy Simpler's squadron arrived in the Pacific, the orderly prewar air group arrangement was long gone. Therefore, VF-5 embarked in *Saratoga* to support Operation Watchtower, the occupation of Guadalcanal. In its first day of combat, 7 August, the squadron intercepted Japanese land-based aircraft from Rabaul, New Britain and claimed 14 victories. However, the F4Fs were roughly treated by combat-experienced Zero pilots, who downed five VF-5 aircraft with the loss of two pilots.

During the Eastern Solomons carrier battle of 24 August, VF-5 was credited with 19 more kills. The following month Simpler took 24 of his Wildcats ashore, operating beside the Marines from Henderson Field and the Fighter Strip. Between 12 September and 15 October, Fighting Five gained 45 more victories while producing three aces: Lt. Hayden Jensen, Lt(jg) Carlton Starkes, and Ens. Weasel Wesolowski.

In mid-October, Simpler began sending most of his exhausted squadron back to the States, staging southward through Espiritu Santo. From August to October, 54 pilots passed through the squadron, with 12 killed or missing. Though some small detachments remained behind temporarily, Fighting Five's contribution to victory at Guadalcanal was ended.

Wartime Cos: Lt.Cdr. N.W. Ellis 3 Apr 41
Lt.Cdr. Wallace M. Beakley 29 Jan 42
Lt.Cdr. Leroy C. Simpler 25 Apr 42

Disestablished: 7 Jan 43

VF-5 (II)

Chronology: established as VF-1 (15 Feb 43)
redesignated VF-5 (15 Jul 43)

Deployments: *Yorktown* (CV-10) Aug 43-Apr 44 F6F-3
Franklin (CV-13) Feb-Mar 45 F4U-1D

Combat record: 93.5 victories, 7 aces. Losses unknown.
Top score: Lt(jg) Robert W. Duncan, 7.

For half a century, the Screaming Eagles were a rock of consistency in a capricious, erratic sea of naval designations. Almost unique among Navy squadrons, Fighting 5 bore the same number for 47 of its 52 years.

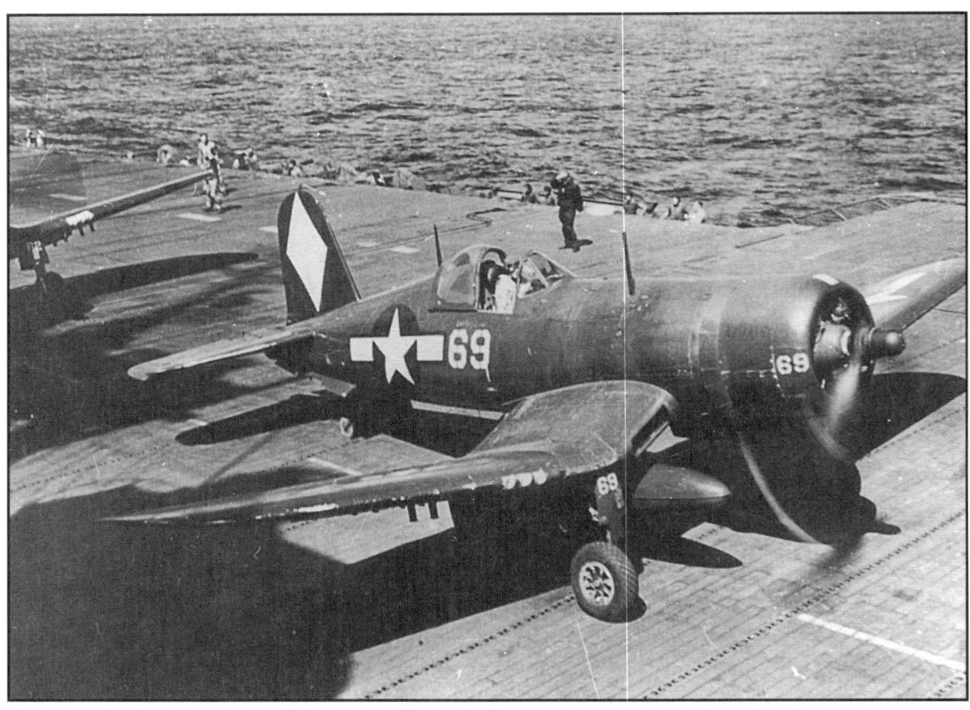

After a 1943-44 Hellcat cruise aboard the second *Yorktown* (CV-10), the second VF-5 re-equipped with Corsairs. This F4U-1D carries *Franklin*'s distinctive diamond tail emblem as it prepares to launch from "Big Ben" during February 1945. The ship and squadron suffered terribly as a result of conventional air attack off Japan on 19 March, victims of the worst damage ever inflicted on a surviving aircraft carrier.

The second VF-5 (designated six months after the first squadron stood down) was among the first to receive Hellcats. Like its predecessor, the new Fighting Five was assigned to a carrier named *Yorktown*—second of the new Essex class. Under skipper Ed Owen and CAG Jim Flatley, VF-5 helped launch the Central Pacific offensive in the summer of 1943, scoring its first 16 victories during the 5 October attack on Wake Island. After the Kwajalein operation in December and January, *Yorktown* played a major role in the first Truk strike, 17 February 1944. From early morning to late afternoon, Fighting Five claimed 30 kills, producing the squadron's first ace in the process—LtJG Bob Duncan.

Another two-day operation against the Palau Islands nearly matched that total on 30-31 March, with 29.5 confirmed. The squadron's final combats of the deployment came near the end of April with missions over Hollandia, New Guinea, and a return to Truk. By 30 April Ed Owens' pilots claimed 93.5 victories.

FitRon Five became one of the few to switch from Hellcats to Corsairs for a second combat cruise. Embarked in *Franklin*, the squadron made a good start with 13 victories from CV-13 on 18 March 1945, attacking Kagoshima Bay, Japan. Another victory came the next morning as CAG Cdr. E.B. Parker, splashed a Judy. But moments later "Big Ben" took two bombs through the packed flight deck, igniting aviation fuel and ordnance.

Wracked by violent fires and explosions, the ship lost most of its aircraft and more than 1,100 casualties. It was the worst toll ever inflicted upon an American aircraft carrier, with 124 KIAs in the air group, but CV-13's determined crew saved their ship.

The squadron reformed at Klamath Falls, Oregon, in May 1945.

Wartime COs:	Lt.Cdr. Charles L. Crommelin	16 Feb 43
	Lt.Cdr. Edward M. Owen	Sep 43
	Cdr. Edwin B. Parker	22 Mar 44
	Lt.Cdr. McGregor Kilpatrick	8 May 45

Subsequent record: redesignated VF-5A (1946), VF-51 (1948). VF-51 become one of the Navy's earliest jet squadrons, and adding kills in Korea and Vietnam. Callously disestablished in 1995.

VF-6 (I) Shooting Stars

Chronology: established as VF-1B (1 Jul 35)
redesignated VF-8B (1937), VF-6 (1937)

Deployments:	*Enterprise* (CV-6)	Dec 41-Aug 42	F4F-3/4
	Saratoga (CV-3)	Dec 42-Feb 43	F4F-4
	Guadalcanal	Feb-Apr 43	F4F-4
	Victorious	Jun-Jul 43	F4F-4

***Enterprise* was known as "the fightingest ship in the U.S. Navy," and VF-6 flew from her through most of 1942. Here F4F-3As pack the deck following the Marcus Island raid of 4 March as ordnancemen disarm the four .50 caliber guns in each Wildcat. The squadron subsequently flew F4F-4s at Midway and Guadalcanal, and traded designations with VF-3 in July 1943. (credit Tailhook Assn.)**

Combat record: 67 victories, one ace. Lost 12 pilots?
Top score: Machinist Donald Runyon, 8 (11).

Fighting Six was *Enterprise's* resident fighter squadron from the first day of the Pacific War. Three Shooting Star pilots were killed trying to land at Pearl Harbor the night of 7 December, shot down by frightened U.S. anti-aircraft gunners.

The Navy's first fighter victory of the war came over Taroa Island on 1 February 1942 when Lt(jg) W.E. Rawie bagged a Nate. Lt. Jim Gray claimed two kills minutes later, and three more fell during the day.

By June, LtCdr Wade McClusky had become *Enterprise* CAG, leaving Gray to assume command of VF-6. During the Midway battle the Shooting Stars claimed nine kills, but the strike escort the morning of 4 June unknowingly tagged onto *Hornet's* VT-8, resulting in loss of communication with Torpedo Six. Shortly after the battle, Lt. Lou Bauer succeeded Gray as CO VF-6.

The Guadalcanal campaign brought repeated aerial combat. In three days of August, Bauer's pilots claimed 47 shootdowns—mainly during the Eastern Solomons carrier duel of the 24th. From these battles Machinist Don Runyon emerged as the Navy's leading ace, with nine victories—a title he held until January 1944.

Transferred to *Saratoga* at year end, "Bauer's Flowers" found slim pickings in the new year. Four Bettys were shot down in February, thus ending the Shooting Stars' victory log.

An unusual "crossdeck" experience occurred when Bauer took his squadron aboard HMS *Victorious* to support the New Georgia landings 20 June to 24 July.

On 15 July VF-6 and Butch O'Hare's VF-3 exchanged numbers—a move intended to realign designations with reality in the carrier air groups. Since VF-6 had been in *Saratoga* (CV-3) and VF-3 in *Enterprise* (CV-6), the numbers had been out of kilter for some months. At any rate, it mattered little to those involved, as Bauer's squadron returned to the U.S. in September.

Wartime COs:	Lt.Cdr. Clarence W. McClusky	27 Jun 41
	Lt. James S. Gray	21 May 42
	Lt. Louis H. Bauer	19 Jun 42

Subsequent record: redesignated VF-3 (15 Jul 43), VF-3A (1946), VF-31 (1948). Still active as the Tomcatters in 1995.

VF-6 (II)

Chronology: established as VF-3 (23 Sep 21)
redesignated VF-2 (1922), VF-6B (1927), VB-2B (1928), VF-6B (1930), VF-3 (1937), VF-6 (15 Jul 43)

Deployments: dets in *Independence* (CVL-22), *Princeton* (CVL-23), *Belleau Wood* (CVL-24), *Cowpens* (CVL-25), *Saratoga* (CV-3) and *Essex* (CV-9) | Aug-Dec 43 | F6F-3
Intrepid (CV-11) | Jan-Feb 44 | F6F-3
Hancock (CV-19) | Mar-Apr, Jun-Sep 45 | F6F-5, -5N

Combat record: 57.66 victories, one ace. Lost 5+ on deployments.
Top score: Lt(jg) Alexander Vraciu, 9 (19)

Aboard *Independence,* CVL-22, in 1943 the "O'Hare Flight" of VF-6 poses: (l to r) Lt. (j.g.) Alex Vraciu, Lt. Cdr. Butch O'Hare, Lt. Sy Mendenhall, and Ens. Willie Callan.

When VF-3 and -6 swapped identities in July 1943, Butch O'Hare continued leading his redesignated squadron with all the professionalism of his prewar VF-3. Though the new Fighting Six soon found itself dispersed among six carriers late that year, the various dets left their mark. Lt(jg) Dick Loesch scored the Hellcat's first victory, splashing an Emily patrol plane near Howland Island on 1 September. Lt(jg) Thad Coleman, a future ace, added a second Kawanishi two days later.

O'Hare had been recognized as the first Navy ace of the war, but waited 20 months for his second combat. Over Wake Island on 5 October he knocked down a Zeke and a Betty while his section leader, LtJG Alex Vraciu, destroyed another Zeke. O'Hare shortly left to become CAG-6 in *Enterprise*, and disappeared during a night interception 26 November. He was succeeded by Lt.Cdr. Stinky Harrison. By year's end VF-6 claimed 14 shootdowns before rejoining the air group in *Intrepid.*

Seven twin-engine planes were splashed near Roi Island on 29 January 1944, including three by Vraciu. Then, during the first Truk raid on 17 February, Fighting Six added 16 more victories, including four by Vraciu who became the squadron's sole ace. When "Evil I" was torpedoed that night, the squadron's first tour came to an end with 37.5 victories by 21 pilots.

After a year's turnaround, VF-6 returned to combat at Okinawa campaign, embarked in *Hancock*. Three probables were claimed off Japan on 18-19 March, but 15 confirmed were added by 6 April. However, damage to the ship forced "Hanna" off the line until June, and only five more aerial victories were scored by 15 August. FitRon Six kept the pressure on the enemy, though,

One of the senior F6F squadrons, VF-6 (originally VF-3) flew a split tour from various CVs and CVLs in 1943-44, then returned aboard *Hancock* in early 1945. This F6F-5 snags one of "Hannah's" arresting wires during operations off Japan in February.

with 61 planes destroyed on the ground 13 August. Top score among the 1945 pilots was Ens. R.L. Bowman with four.

Wartime COs:	Lt.Cdr. Edward H. O'Hare	15 Jul 43
	Lt.Cdr. Harry W. Harrison, Jr.	11 Oct 43
	Lt.Cdr. Ralph L. Copeland	23 Aug 44
	Lt.Cdr. Roland W. Schumann, Jr.	28 May 45

Disestablished: 29 Oct 45

VBF-6 Whistling Death

Established: 2 Jan 45

Deployment: *Hancock* (CV-19) Mar-Apr 45; Jun-Sep 45 F4U-4

Combat record: 17 victories. Lost 10 pilots on deployment.
Top score: Lt. A.G. Becker and Lt(jg) R.S. Farnsworth, 2 each.

Established at Hilo, Hawaii, VBF-6 was formed in time to deploy in *Hancock* for strikes against Japan prior to the Okinawa invasion. Pacific combat was nothing new to the skipper, as Lt. Cdr. Bud Schumann had been CO of VF-10 during the Grim Reapers' F6F deployment the previous year.

Among the first fighting-bombing squadrons established was VBF-6, which entered combat shortly after establishment in January 1945. This F4U-1D nosed up after landing aboard Hancock on 4 April 1945.

First blood for the Whistling Death squadron was dawn on the morning of 18 March, the day before *Franklin* sustained appalling damage in a conventional bombing attack. *Hancock's* Corsairs helped cap the stricken "Big Ben" until the 21st, when she drew out of range of the Japanese homeland.

The F4Us' busiest air-to-air segment of the cruise occurred when Schumann's pilots claimed eight victories at the height of the *kamikaze* campaign, 3-7 April. However, Hanna herself was damaged on the latter date, not returning to WestPac until early June.

Only three more victories were logged before the cease-fire: two kills on 25 June and a Kate on 15 August. The latter, by Lt(jg) Bob Farnsworth, was one of the last five aerial victories of the war.

Wartime CO:	Lt.Cdr. Roland W. Schumann, Jr.	2 Jan 45
	Lt.Cdr. Lavell M. Bigelow	28 May 45

Disestablished: 29 Oct 45

VF-7

Established: 3 Jan 44

Deployment: *Hancock* (CV-19) Sep 44-Jan 45 F6F-3, -5, -5N, -5P

Combat record: 72 victories, 2 aces. Lost 29 pilots on deployment.
Top score: Lt.Cdr. Leonard J. Check, 10.

A Grumman F6F Hellcat of VF-7 late in 1944 aboard *Hancock,* bears the squadron's distinctive horseshoe tail marking.

Fighting Seven stood up at Atlantic City on the third day of 1944, remaining in Atlantic City for part of its early training. The squadron arrived in the Western Pacific in early October 1944, just as the Philippine campaign was beginning. The first combat occurred over Formosa on the 12th, as four Japanese fighters and a Jill were destroyed. The next two days brought four more confirmed.

By far the biggest day in combat was 29 October, with fighter sweeps over Luzon and CAPs protecting the task force. During a ForceCAP that afternoon, Lt.Cdr. Check downed four Zekes while his pilots claimed 17.5 more during the day. Additional combat came in the Philippines during November and December.

The skipper was lost over Formosa on 4 January, killed in a midair collision. He was succeeded by Lt. John Duncan.

Fighting Seven's last combat occurred 21 January, again in the Formosa area. The only other ace was Lt. Johnnie Bridges, with six victories aboard *Hancock* plus a shared previously with VF-6 in early 1943. In all, 37 pilots shared in the credited 72 victories.

Wartime COs:	Lt.Cdr. Leonard J. Check +	3 Jan 44
	Lt. John A. Duncan	4 Jan 45
	Lt.Cdr. Onia B. Stanley, Jr.	27 Mar 45

Disestablished: 8 Jun 46

VF-8 (I)

Established: 2 Sep 41

Deployment: *Hornet* (CV-8) Dec 41-Jun 42 F4F-4

Combat record: 5 victories. Lost 3 pilots on deployment.
Top score: Ens. Morrill I. Cook, 2.

The first Fighting Eight was part of the original *Hornet's* ill-starred air group. The squadron logged one day of combat—4 June at Midway—and came off poorly even by CV-8's tragic standards.

While Torpedo Eight flew independently to the Japanese carrier force, the rest of the air group searched in vain for a target. The CAG, Cdr. Stanhope Ring, led 35 SBDs and 10 of Lt.Cdr. Pat Mitchell's Wildcats on a prolonged, fuel-guzzling flight before belatedly breaking off the hunt. All of Mitchell's F4Fs splashed with empty tanks, and two pilots were lost in the process. The rest were picked up days later.

Meanwhile, other VF-8 pilots on CAP helped intercept *Hiryu's* dive-bombing attack on *Yorktown*. Four *Hornet* Wildcats were credited with five shootdowns, including two Zeroes by Ens. Morrill Cook, Jr. Tragically, another Fighting Eight pilot was killed by U.S. anti-aircraft fire.

With Mitchell missing and his exec reporting to sick bay, VF-8 badly needed leadership. Lt.Cdr. John S. Thach arrived on the 5th with elements of his own mixed VF-3/42 and operated from *Hornet* for the rest of the battle.

Part of *Hornet*'s (CV-8) ill-fated air group, the first VF-8's combat was limited to Midway, when the F4F pilots claimed five victories in exchange for three pilots lost and 11 aircraft—nearly all to operational causes. This F4F-3, photographed near Norfolk in February 1942, bears the markings of Lt.Cdr. S.G. "Pat" Mitchell, who commanded the squadron from establishment in September 1941 through the Battle of Midway.

Despite its failings at Midway, some of VF-8's junior officers later made distinguished records. Henry Carey and Jock Sutherland returned to *Hornet* with VF-72 in time for Santa Cruz, and added to their scores with VF-10. George Formanek and John Magda became standouts later in the war. Formanek was killed over New Guinea with VF-30 and Magda, a Blue Angel leader, died in Korea in 1951.

Cdrs. Ring and Mitchell both retired as admirals.

Wartime CO: Lt.Cdr. Samuel G. Mitchell 2 September 41

Disestablished: 28 Aug 42

VF-8 (II)

Established: 1 Jun 43

Deployment: *Bunker Hill* (CV-17) Mar-Oct 44 F6F-3, -3P, -5, -5P

Combat record: 156 victories, 13 aces. Lost 7 on deployment.
Top score: Cdr. William M. Collins, 9.

The second VF-8 was vastly more successful than the first. Flying from *Bunker Hill,* Cdr. W.M. Collins' squadron claimed 156 kills in the Marianas and Philippine campaigns. Here *Bunker Hill* F6F-3s are being armed for an offensive mission against Saipan in June 1944

Established at Norfolk in mid-1943, the second VF-8 was led by 32-year-old Cdr. William M. Collins from the Annapolis class of '34. He benefitted from combat-experienced pilots such as Lt.Cdr. Scott McCuskey (VF-42 and VF-3) and Lt(jg) Whitey Feightner (VF-10).

The squadron's baptism came during strikes on the Palaus on 30-31 March 1944, when 11 victories were claimed. Two more during the second Truk raid on 29 April were the last until the Marianas campaign.

On 11 June, VF-8 notched seven more kills during CAPs and strikes against Guam. The carrier battle of the 19th resulted in widespread opportunity, as *Bunker Hill* Hellcats splashed 20 raiders, nearly all before noon. The next evening's attack on the Japanese task force resulted in two confirmed and two probables.

Fighting Eight shone during September and October battles over the Philippines and Formosa. Twenty-two claims resulted from day-long combats over Luzon on 21 September, eclipsed by a startling 50 at Formosa on 12 October. Five of those fell to the CO; 13 more were splashed in the next two days.

VF-8 ended its combat deployment with a Frances snooper dispatched on 21 October. The squadron reformed at Alameda, California, in January 1945 and was preparing for a second combat cruise when the war ended.

Wartime COs:	Cdr. William M. Collins, Jr.	1 Jun 43
	Lt.Cdr. Paul D. Duke	1 Jan 45

Disestablished: 23 Nov 45

VF-9 Cat o' Nines/Hellcats

Established: 1 Mar 42

Deployments:	*Ranger* (CV-4)	Nov 42	F4F-4
	Essex (CV-9)	Mar 43-Nov 44	F6F-3
	Lexington (CV-16)	Feb-Mar 45	F6F-5, -5N, -5P
	Yorktown (CV-10)	Mar-Jun 45.	F6F-5, -5N, -5P

Combat record: 256.75 victories, 20 aces. Lost 16 officers, 2 EM.
Top score: Lt. Eugene A. Valencia, 23.

One of the longest-serving squadrons of the war, VF-9 also was one of the few to engage two Axis powers. During its first brief cruise, flying F4Fs from *Ranger*, Fighting Nine claimed six Vichy French fighters over Morocco in November 1942. Before year end Jack Raby's gang was back on the East Coast, becoming the first to receive F6F-3 Hellcats.

Under Lt.Cdr. Phil Torrey, Fighting Nine rode *Essex* to the Western Pacific and began bagging Japanese planes 11 months after Operation Torch in North Africa. The CO was first to score against Japan, downing one of four Zekes the squadron claimed at Wake Island on 5 October 1943. The next event was vastly grander in scale, as land-based enemy aircraft attacked the U.S.

Lt. Gene Valencia's division aboard *Lexington* (CV-16) and *Yorktown* (CV-10) during 1945, with an aggregate 50 confirmed kills. From left: Valencia (23), Lt(jg)s Clinton Smith (6), Harris Mitchell (10), and Jim French (11).

carrier force off Rabaul, New Britain, on 11 November. Over a five-hour period the Hellcats were credited with 55 shootdowns.

By the first Truk raid in February 1944, Lt(jg) Mac McWhorter was not only the first F6F ace, but the first F6F double ace. On 17 February VF-9 splashed 35 fighters and floatplanes inside Truk lagoon, adding 11 more at Saipan on the 22nd. By the end of cruise, 120 meatballs adorned the Hellcats' scoreboard.

VF-9 eturned to combat 12 months later, under Lt.Cdr. Herb Houck. Briefly flying from *Lexington*, the air group participated in the Tokyo strikes of 16 February. In all, 28 victories were claimed during the day, though Houck was lost. Lt. Jack Kitchen then assumed command.

Shifting to *Yorktown*, VF-9 made its presence felt throughout the Okinawa campaign. Events peaked on 4 May as the Hellcats claimed 30.75 shootdowns, followed by 22 on the 11th. At this time Lt. Gene Valencia's division became the most successful combat team in Navy history, downing 43 planes without serious damage to themselves. Additionally, Lt. Marv Franger kept his string going as the only Navy ace with confirmed kills in three consecutive deployments for a total of nine. VF-9 finished the war as the third-ranking FitRon in the Navy.

Wartime COs:	Lt.Cdr. John A. Raby	1 Mar 42
	Lt.Cdr. Philip H. Torrey	14 Aug 43
	Lt.Cdr. Herbert N. Houck +	24 Dec 43
	Lt. John S. Kitchen	17 Feb 45

Disestablished: 28 Sep or 15 Oct 45

VBF-9

Established: 6 Jan 45

Deployment:			
	Lexington (CV-16)	Feb-Mar 45	F6F-5
	Yorktown (CV-10)	Mar-Jun 45	F6F-5

Combat record: 51 victories, one ace. Lost 6 pilots on deployment.
Top score: Lt. Edgar B. McClure, 5.

When authorization for establishment of VBF squadrons came through in January 1945, VF-9 was already at Ponam Air Base, Manus Islands, in the Western Pacific. Therefore, Lt.Cdr. Frank Lawlor took half of the squadron and stood up the fighter-bomber outfit on the spot. The first three victories occurred during the first day of the Tokyo strikes, 16 February, flying from *Lexington*.

Most subsequent combat was aboard Yorktown, with activity of varying intensity during April and May. In all, 37 of the squadron's 51 victories were claimed during the *kamikaze* crisis of April, with 10 splashed on the 29th alone. Six more fell during May and the last victim, a Tony, was downed on 6 June, just before CVG-9 completed its tour.

The cruise produced one ace, Lt. Edgar McClure, while two other pilots—Lt. John Snyder and Lt(jg) Gene Walker—downed four bandits each.

Wartime CO: Lt.Cdr. Frank L. Lawlor 6 Jan 45

Disestablished: 15 Oct or 5 Nov 45

VF-10 Grim Reapers

Established: 3 Jun 42

Deployments:			
	Enterprise (CV-6)	Oct 42-Feb 43	F4F-4
	Enterprise	Jan-Jul 44	F6F-3
	Intrepid (CV-11)	Feb-Apr 45	F4U-1D
	Intrepid	Jul-Sep 45	F4U-4

Combat record: 217 victories, 13 aces. Lost 26 on deployments.
Top score: Lt. Philip R. Kirkwood, 12.

The Grim Reapers held a unique spot in U.S. Navy history: they were the only squadron to fly combat tours in Wildcats, Hellcats, and Corsairs. Established at San Diego in June 1942, VF-10 was led by the combat-experienced Jim Flatley, recently returned from the Coral Sea battle as exec of VF-42. Recruiting all the talent possible, he signed on such SBD experts as John Leppla and Swede Vejtasa. The former was KIA at Santa Cruz; the latter possibly saved *Enterprise* by splashing seven bombers that same day.

VF-10 Grim Reapers in their *Enterprise* ready room after the first Truk raid, 17 February 1944. Debriefing with CO Killer Kane (far right) are aces Frenchy Reulet (seated second from left), Phil Kirkwood (on the deck) and Flash Gordon (next to Kane). Kirkwood, with a total of 12 victories in the F6F and F4U cruises, emerged as the squadron's top ace.

The first of six combat days during the Reapers' initial cruise was the carrier battle of 26 October. During day-long operations off the Santa Cruz Islands, Flatley's pilots claimed 21 kills, including seven by Vejtasa.

With *Enterprise* too valuable to risk close to shore, VF-10 flew into Guadalcanal in mid-November, claiming 10 victories from the 13th to the 15th. Back aboard the Big E in January, Fighting 10 claimed 11 Bettys (three by Whitey Feightner) defending the crippled cruiser *Chicago* (CA-29) on 30 January. By the end of the first cruise the Reapers claimed 43 victories.

Flatley's former exec, W.R. "Killer" Kane, took VF-10 back aboard The Big E following her refit in Bremerton, Wash. That deployment, in Hellcats, logged 88.5 shootdowns including 29 over Truk on 17 Feb 44 and 19 in the Marianas Turkey Shoot, 19 Jun 44.

Transitioned to Corsairs under VF-5 vet Wally Clarke, the Reapers boarded *Intrepid* for their third deployment in February 1945, entering combat in March. They quickly hit their stride, scoring 87 kills in March and April—nearly as many as on their entire second cruise. Of these, 33 were claimed during the major *kamikaze* attacks of 16 April, with Lt(jg) Phil Kirkwood and Ens. Alfred Lerch gunning six and seven, respectively. However, that day the suiciders took their revenge, forcing "Evil I" out of action. She only returned to WestPac in July but launched no more strikes until 6 August. Hostilities ceased nine days later.

Wartime COs:	Lt.Cdr. James H. Flatley	3 Jun 42
	Lt.Cdr. William R. Kane	13 Feb 43
	Lt. Roland W. Schumann, Jr.	Feb 44
	Lt.Cdr. Wilmer E. Rawie	15 Sep 44
	Lt.Cdr. Walter E. Clarke	19 Jan 45

Disestablished: 26 Nov 45

VBF-10

Established: 2 Jan 45

Deployment: *Intrepid* (CV-11) Feb-Apr, Jul-Sep 45   F4U-1D, -4

Combat record: 15 victories. Losses unknown.
Top score: Ens. Raymond V. Lanthier, Jr., 3.

VBF-10 got off to a strong start with an experienced skipper. Lt.Cdr. W.E. Rawie had flown Wildcats with VF-6 aboard *Enterprise* early in the war, then reformed the Reapers after their F6F cruise. He transferred to the BomFitRon when it was established and led the unit for the rest of the war. Air Group 10 thus became one of the few whose two fighter squadrons both flew Corsairs.

First blood for the squadron was drawn by CAG-10, Cdr. John Hyland, who splashed a floatplane fighter over Kure Harbor on 19 March. Three other pilots also scored in the same combat.

Operations switched to the Ryukyus in early April, where VBF-10 claimed two more kills on the 7th. The squadron's last day of air-to-air combat came during the major suicide raids of the 16th, as nine planes were destroyed. However, *Intrepid* was badly damaged that day and steamed to the west coast for repairs.

Re-equipped with new F4U-4s, VBF-10 was back at work in July but had no further opportunity for aerial engagements.

Wartime CO: Lt.Cdr. Wilmer E. Rawie 2 Jan 45

Disestablished: 26 Nov 45

VF-11 Sundowners

Established: 1 Aug 42

Deployments:	Guadalcanal	May-Jul 43	F4F-4
	Hornet (CV-12)	Oct 44-Jan 45	F6F-3, -5, -5N, -5P

Combat record: 158 victories, 7 aces. Lost 23 plus 2 POWs.
Top score: Lt. Charles R. Stimpson, 16.

One of Naval Aviation's most enduring symbols was the Sundowner emblem: two stubby Grummans shooting a red sun into the blue ocean against a yellow sky. It adorned Navy fighters for most of the 52 years that VF-11/111 existed.

Formed at North Island, Air Group 11 was intended to go aboard *Hornet* (CV-8) sometime late in 1942. Her loss at Santa Cruz changed all that, so the four squadrons flew from Guadalcanal in the summer of 1943. While there the Sundowners claimed 52 victories, producing the Navy's first land-based ace in a day: Ens. Vern Graham. Lt(jg) Charlie Stimpson claimed six kills and Jim Swope 4.66.

Upon reforming on the West Coast, VF-11 proceeded to Hawaii and boarded *Hornet* in the fall of 1944. The new skipper was Gene Fairfax, a noted Annapolis boxer and former OS2U pilot who scored four kills in Hellcats.

First blood of the deployment came on 10 October, inaugurating three months of combat over the Philippines, Formosa, and Hong Kong. In a lopsided dogfight off Formosa on the 14th, the Sundowners splashed 18 bandits, including five by Charlie Stimpson. Four days later 19 more victories were claimed over Clark Field. The squadron's best day was in the same area, 5 November, when the Sundowners bested 25 Japanese fighters, mostly army types.

Three of VF-11's seven aces grab a snack in *Hornet*'s (CV-12) pantry during late 1944. From left: Lt.Jim Swope, Lt. Charlie Stimpson, and Lt(jg) Blake Moranville. Stimpson was one of only four aces in both the Wildcat and Hellcat, while Swope had 4.66 victories in F4Fs and five in F6Fs. "Rabbit" Moranville was shot down and captured by the Vichy French during January 1945 strikes over Indochina and walked to safety with a Foreign Legion troop.

During strikes on French Indochina 12 January 1945, Lt(jg) Blake Moranville was shot down by flak. He became one of only two Navy aces captured during the war, but evaded the Japanese when former Vichy forces switched sides. In all, the second tour netted 103 more victories as Stimpson retained his top spot by adding 10 Hellcat victories.

Wartime COs:	Lt.Cdr. Charles R. Fenton	10 Oct 42
	Lt.Cdr. Charles M. White	20 Apr 43
	Cdr. Gordon D. Cady	25 Sep 43
	Lt.Cdr. Eugene G. Fairfax	15 Aug 44
	Lt.Cdr. P.W. Jackson	21 Apr 45

Subsequent record: Redesignated VF-11A (1946) and VF-111 (1948). The Sundowners made three cruises and scored the Navy's first jet victory during the Korean War. Though disestablished in February 1959, the unit's designation was immediately shifted to VA-156, and the Sundowner/VF-111 identification remained until final stand-down in 1995.

VGF-11

Chronology: Established as VGF-11 (5 Aug 42?)
Redesignated VC-11 (1 Mar 43), VF-21 (16 May 43)

Deployments: Guadalcanal May-Jul 43 F4F-4

Combat record: 10 victories as VGF-11,

See VF-21 for complete history.

VF-12 Corsairs/Thunderbirds

Established: 9 Jan 42

Deployments:	*Saratoga* (CV-3)	Aug-Sep 43	F6F-3
	Guadalcanal	Sep 43	F6F-3
	Saratoga	Oct 43-Jun 44	F6F-3
	Randolph (CV-15)	Jan-Jun 45	F6F-5, -5, -5N, -5P

Combat record: 71 victories, 2 aces. Lost 10 on deployments.
Top scores: Lt.Cdr. Frederick H. Michaelis, 5, and Lt. Harold E. Vita, 5 (6).

Established at San Diego, Jumpin' Joe Clifton's VF-12 received the Navy's first F4U-1s in October 1942. Despite training losses with the Corsair, the squadron was devoted to the type and took its F4Us to the Pacific in the summer of 1943. However, VF-12 was required to exchange its Corsairs for Hellcats before deploying in *Saratoga* that August.

The squadron's major combat was the Rabaul strikes of November 1943, with 12 victories credited on the 5th. Later under Lt.Cdr. Bob Dose´, VF-12 cross-decked with HMS *Victorious* and finished the cruise with 20 victories. Four belonged to Lt. Johnny Magda, later a Blue Angels leader.

The second cruise Fighting 12 benefited from aces and other combat veterans of VF-9 John Franks, Mac McWhorter, and Hal Vita. Inaugurating *Randolph* to combat, the new VF-12 claimed 14 kills during over-water interceptions on 16 February 1945. Operations against the Tokyo Plain continued briefly the next day, with two more victories.

A return to Japan on the 25th resulted in seven more victories, after which the scene shifted to Okinawa. South of Kikai Shima on 17 April, VF-12 claimed a dozen Japanese fighters, with six more victories by month's end. By 14 May the tally had risen to 51. However, what the Japanese could not accomplish was finally done in June, when a P-38 crashed on the flight deck while buzzing Ulithi lagoon. Air Group 12 was on its way home, courtesy of the Army Air Force.

FitRon 12's skipper and only ace, Mike Michaelis, retired as a four-star admiral, widely admired in the naval service.

Wartime COs:	Lt.Cdr. Joseph C. Clifton	12 Feb 43
	Lt.Cdr. Robert G. Dose´	Jan 44
	Cdr. Noel A.M. Gayler	20 Jul 44
	Lt.Cdr. Frederick H. Michaelis	9 Feb 45

Disestablished: 27 Sep 45

Though formed as the first F4U squadron, VF-12 exchanged Corsairs for Hellcats in mid-1943. The second cruise, in *Randolph*, involved missions against Japan and Okinawa during 1945. Cdr. Charlie Crommelin's air group benefited from several VF-9 veterans, including aces Rube Denoff and Chick Smith. This photo shows "Randy's" distinctive tail stripe markings.

VBF-12

Established: 2 Jan 45

Deployment: *Randolph* (CV-15) Jan-Jun 45 F6F-5

Combat record: 74 victories, two aces. No combat losses.
Top scores: Lt. Alfred G. Bolduc and Ens. Delmar K. Johannsen, 5 each

When established from the cadre of VF-12, the fighter-bombers inherited a strong pool of talent. Combat veterans included Matt Byrnes, Rube Denoff, Lou Menard, and Armistead "Chick" Smith (all of VF-9), plus Danny Carmichael, late of VF-2.

First combat for the air group was the curtain-raiser attack on Honshu in February 1945. Ed Pawka's squadron claimed 26 victories on the 16th and two more the next day. When Pawka moved up to air group commander, he was relieved by Rube Denoff, who added three victories to his previous two with Fighting Nine. His exec was Chick Smith, who became a double ace as a result of both Pacific deployments.

Most of April and May involved CAPs off Okinawa, with VBF-12 frequently in combat. Twenty-three bandits were splashed during four days in April, and 25 more during four days in May. The last victory was an enemy "utility biplane" shot down off Okinawa on 14 May.

Ironically, neither of the squadron's two aces scored on the unit's best day, 16 February. Lt. Al Bolduc downed five planes in two combats, 14 April and 4 May, while Ens. Delmar Johannsen splashed five on 4 and 14 May.

The air group's tour was cut short by *Randolph's* damage at Ulithi in June.

Wartime CO:	Lt.Cdr. Edward J. Pawka	2 Jan 45
	Lt. Reuben H. Denoff	12 May 45

Disestablished: 17 Sep 45

VF-13 Black Cats

Established: 2 Nov 43

Deployment: *Franklin* (CV-13) Mar-Nov 44 F6F-3, -5, -5N, -5P

Combat record: 86 victories, 3 aces. Lost 11 pilots on deployment.
Top score: Ens. Albert J. Pope, 7.

Air Group 13 was constituted in November 1942, but a year would pass before the squadrons became a reality. Even so, CVG-13 was the last air group mated numerically to its carrier's hull number—the common prewar practice. *Franklin* was commissioned in January 1944, and though the air group began workups in March, first combat was delayed until July.

VF-13's first victories occurred during the Fourth of July strikes on the Bonins, with four victories logged west of Iwo Jima. Further operations against the Bonins and Palaus raised the Black Cats' total to 18 by the end of August, at which time the squadron was the first with F6F-5s.

The remainder of the deployment was spent in Formosan and Philippine waters. The squadron's biggest day was 15 October when 20 victories were claimed—nearly all during a morning mission over Manila. Two days later Ens. Nick Smith became the first Black Cat ace, with Ens. Al Pope and the CO, Cdr. Coleman, attaining their fifth victories on the 19th and 24th, respectively.

The final bandits were splashed on the 28th, but two days later a pair of suiciders got through the CAP. One went for *Belleau Wood*; the other for *Franklin*. Both died as they intended, with "Big Ben" sustaining more than 100 casualties with 33 planes destroyed. Cdr. Coleman left *Franklin* to become CAG-18 on 11 November and was succeeded by Lt. J.M. Sullivan.

Fighting 13 lost 11 pilots killed in action and at least three more in operational accidents.

Wartime CO:	Lt.Cdr. T.B. Bradbury	2 Nov 43
	Cdr. Wilson M. Coleman	17 Nov 43
	Lt. Jaye M. Sullivan	11 Nov 44

Disestablished: 20 Oct 45

VF-14 Iron Angels

Established: 1 Sep 43

Deployment: *Wasp* (CV-18) Jan-Nov 44 F6F-3, -5, -5P

Combat record: 146 victories, 8 aces. Lost 20 on deployment.
Top score: Lt. William M. Knight, 7.5.

The Iron Angels logged nearly a year aboard the second *Wasp*, with seven months of combat. First blood was drawn near Marcus Island on 19 May when Lt.Cdr. Biros' division bagged a Betty.

The first large-scale combat occurred 19 June during the Turkey Shoot off Guam and Saipan. During the day the Angels splashed 11.5 raiders, then added six more during the next evening's frantic attack on the Japanese Mobile Fleet. However, *Wasp's* strike diverted to the enemy oiler group, thereby missing the greater portion of Vice Adm. Ozawa's CAP.

Fifteen more kills were claimed during the 4 July mission to Iwo Jima, but more than two months passed before the next opportunity. Strikes against Cebu and Negros Islands in the Philippines on 12 September yielded nine victories by the fighters. However, in an unusual move, several SB2C pilots had transitioned to F6Fs, scoring eight kills over Negros Island. Though scored in Hellcats, these victories were credited to Bombing 14.

The Angels added ten more during strikes on Takao, Formosa, 30 days later. However, by then Lt. Cdr. Biros had been killed, temporarily replaced by Lt. Q.P. Punnell (KIA 25 July) and Lt. Cdr. R. Gray, who was detached in November.

The Iron Angels' single best day of the war was 15 October. While Task Group 38.1 covered the withdrawal of two damaged cruisers from Formosan waters, Japanese aircraft came out in swarms. VF-14 splashed 30.5, raising four pilots to acedom.

Among six victories on 26 October were two Helens off Mindoro Island by Lt (jg) Harold Newell's section. Newell destroyed the first bomber, carrying Warrant Officer Hiroyhoshi Nishizawa to his death. "The Devil" had claimed between 86 and 147 victories – a vastly inflated total, but still indicative of Nishizawa's worth.

Fighting 14 had two other notable days over the Philippines. Sixteen bandits were claimed at Mabalacat Airfield on the 18th, including five by Lt. E.B. Turner. No fewer than 21 fell around Clark Field on 5 November – the day the Angels lost their leading ace when Lt. Knight failed to return. With one more victory the next day, Fighting 14's long war was over.

Wartime COs:	Lt. Cdr Edmund W. Biros+	5 Sep 43
	Lt. J.H. Boyum	20 Jul 44
	Lt. Cdr. R. Gray	16 Aug 44
	Lt. Cdr. H.H. Hassenfratz	2 Nov 44
	Lt. Cdr. F.P. Jacobs	1 Jan 45

Disestablished: 14 Jun 46

VF-15 Fighting Aces

Established: 1 Sep 43

Deployment: *Essex* (CV-9) May-Nov 44 F6F-3/5

Combat record: 310 victories, 26 aces. Lost 20 on deployment.
Top score: Cdr. David McCampbell, 34.

When Cdr. Dave McCampbell stood up VF-15 in September 1943, he set in motion the single most successful deployment for a fighter squadron in U.S. Navy history. Workups aboard *Hornet* (CV-12) on the east coast were marked by a stormy relationship with the carrier's mercurial skipper, Capt. Miles Browning, who relieved the original CAG. McCampbell fleeted up and was relieved by Cdr. Charles Brewer, one year junior to McCampbell at Annapolis.

Combat began in May 1944, embarked in *Essex*, with a far more convivial relationship between ship and air group. Following "warmup" strikes against Marcus Island, VF-15 shot down eight Japanese planes on 11 June, first day of the Marianas operation. Among those scoring were McCampbell, wingman Lt(jg) Roy Rushing, Cdr. Brewer, his exec, Lt.Cdr. Jim Rigg, and Lt. Bert Morris—erstwhile film star and McCampbell's nephew by marriage.

On 19 June the Fighting Aces set a fleet record with 68.5 confirmed kills at the height of the Turkey Shoot. McCampbell scored seven times in two flights; Brewer became an ace in a day, only to be killed that afternoon; while Lt(jg) George Carr also splashed five. Brewer was succeeded by Lt.Cdr. Rigg.

After a two-month drought, the pace picked up with operations over the Philippines. On 12 September the squadron claimed 27 kills, with five by Rigg. Thirty more fell the next day

On 12 October VF-15 became only the second FitRon (after VF-2) to reach 200 victories. Then, on the 24th, the squadron claimed 43 victories during strike escort and CAP. McCampbell and Rushing were credited with nine and six kills, respectively, while two other aces bagged four each. The next day Air Group 15 helped sink four Japanese carriers off Cape Engano, the last time CV aircraft sank flattops in the open sea.

Over Manila Bay on 14 November, McCampbell scored his 34th victory, and the squadron's 310th. With 25 aces (six in double digits), the Fighting Aces more than lived up to their name. Among the notables was Lt. John Symmes, previously of VF-21, one of only four pilots to make ace in the F4F and F6F.

Fighting 15 established the one-tour record for Navy and Marine Corps fighter squadrons, claiming 310 shootdowns between May and November 1944, with 26 aces. "Fabled 15" was aboard *Essex* for both the Marianas campaign and Leyte Gulf—an opportunity afforded few other squadrons. This group portrait, taken on CV-9's hangar deck, probably was posed in October or November with CAG Dave McCampbell's *Minsi III* as a backdrop.

Wartime COs:	Cdr. David McCampbell	1 Sep 43
	Cdr. Charles W. Brewer +	9 Feb 44
	Lt.Cdr. James F. Rigg	19 Jun 44
	Lt.Cdr. George C. Duncan	15 Jan 45
	Lt.Cdr. Gordon E. Firebaugh	25 Feb 45

Disestablished: 20 Oct 45

VF-16 Pistol-Packin' Airdales

Established: 16 Nov 42

Deployments:	*Lexington* (CV-16)	Sep 43-Jun 44	F6F-3
	Randolph (CV-15)	Jun-Sep 45	F6F-5, -5N, -5P

Combat record: 154.5 victories, 9 aces. Losses unknown.
Top score: Lt(jg) Alex Vraciu, 10 (19)

Established at Quonset Point, R.I., VF-16 was mated with *Lexington* (CV-16) in one of the most significant of all early Hellcat deployments. The Airdales' first combat came at Wake Island, 5 October 1943, with six Zekes destroyed. They were followed by a two-day blitz in the Gilberts when Cdr. Paul Buie's pilots claimed 29 victories on 23-24 November, including five by Lt(jg) Ralph Hanks, who became the first F6F ace in a day.

Lt.Cdr. Paul Buie, skipper of VF-16, briefs nine of his Airedales on *Lexington*'s (CV-16) flight deck circa November 1943.

Subsequent combat at Kwajalein, Truk, and Hollandia ran the squadron tally to 86 before opening of the Marianas campaign in early June 1944. By then Lt(jg) Alex Vraciu had reported aboard, already with nine victories from VF-6. During the day-long Japanese air strikes against Task Force 58, the Airdales splashed 46 bandits, including six Judy dive bombers by Vraciu. He added another victory, his 19th, during the long-range strike on the Japanese fleet the next afternoon to become the Navy's top ace.

It was a VF-16 pilot, Lt(jg) Ziggy Neff, who probably coined the phrase "turkey shoot" in context of the Philippine Sea battle.

At the end of the deployment in June, VF-16 held the record for carrier fighter squadrons, with 136.5 victories.

Returning to WestPac in *Randolph*, FitRon 16 found aerial combat on only five days of the 1945 cruise. Thirteen of the 18 victories in that deployment were claimed on 28 July. On that day, Lts. John Bartol and Cleveland Null logged their fifth victories during combats over Ozuki. Both were second-tour pilots; Bartol's first kills dated from October 43, and Null's from December of that year. The Airdales thereby produced two of the last three Navy aces of the Second World War.

Wartime COs:	Cdr. Paul D. Buie	16 Nov 42
	Lt.Cdr C.S. Moffett	25 Aug 44

Disestablished: 6 Nov 45

VBF-16

Established: 3 Jan 45

Deployment: *Randolph* (CV-15) Jun-Sep 45 F6F-5

Combat record: 1 victory. Lost 3 pilots on deployment.
Top score: Lt(jg) E.C. Murray.

VBF-16 was among the first fighting-bombing squadrons established when the VF/VBF split was authorized in January 1945. Six months later the air group embarked in *Randolph*, participating in the final phase of the Pacific war. From June through mid-August strikes and CAPs were flown over and around the enemy home islands, but aerial opposition was negligible. With Japan hoarding its forces against the certainty of invasion by year end, few sightings and fewer shootdowns were logged.

The squadron's only two claims occurred near the end of the cruise. On 30 July a Nell was probably splashed near Ashikaga, while on 13 August a Myrt reconnaissance plane was confirmed destroyed near the task force.

Wartime CO: Lt.Cdr. E.A. Kraft 2 Jan 45

Disestablished: 6 Nov 45

VF-17 Jolly Rogers

Established: 1 Jan 43

Deployments:	Solomons	Oct 43-Mar 44	F4U-1, -1A
	Hornet (CV-12)	Feb-Jun 45	F6F-5, -5P

Combat record: 313 victories, 23 aces. Lost 17 pilots deployed.
Top score: Lt(jg) Ira Kepford, 16.

The Navy's highest-scoring fighting squadron actually was two separate units with the same designation. However, from the genealogical viewpoint, the lineage was direct.

Lt.Cdr. Tom Blackburn established VF-17 as the Navy's second F4U squadron on New Year's Day 1943. After turning the Corsair into a suitable carrier aircraft, the Jolly Rogers sailed for the Pacific aboard *Bunker Hill* with the rest of Air Group 17, arriving in Hawaii that fall. However, insufficient Corsair parts in the carrier supply system forced "Blackburn's Irregulars" off the ship, to be replaced by the Hellcats of VF-18.

Sent to the Solomon Islands in October, Fighting 17 operated from Ondonga, New Georgia, until year end, then from the Piva Yoke strip on Bougainville. A brief reunion with *Bunker Hill* occurred during the carrier strike on Rabaul 11 November, when the F4Us landed aboard to refuel and rearm after helping repel a land-based air attack. The 18.5 kills credited that day remained a high for the duration of the first deployment.

Lt(jg) Ike Kepford became the Navy's first triple ace on 19 February 1944, and remained "top gun" until June. At the end of the tour, Blackburn's pilots included 11 aces, and the 152 victories remained the Navy's top Corsair score.

Reforming on the West Coast, Lt.Cdr. Marsh Beebe (like Blackburn, a former CVE pilot) trained a new VF-17 in the F6F, but still sporting the pirate flag. They entered combat from *Hornet* during the spectacular Tokyo strikes, when the Jolly Rogers resumed scoring on 16 February 1945—three days less

Lt(jg) Ike Kepford's No. 29, the most famous Corsair of all. By numerical designation VF-17 was the top Navy fighter squadron of WW II, with 313 confirmed kills. Originally under Lt.Cdr. Tom Blackburn, the Jolly Rogers F4Us claimed 152 victories in the Solomons during 1943-44. After reforming with F6Fs under Lt.Cdr. Marsh Beebe, FitRon 17 deployed in Hornet during 1945 and added another 161. Though sharing the same genaeology, they were two different squadrons with no duplication of personnel.

A Hellcat of VF-17 taxis into position on *Hornet*.

one year after their last Corsair victory. However, their biggest days came over Kanoya on 18 March and near Okinawa on 16 April, with 31 kills on both occasions. The skipper and Lt. Bob Coats became aces in a day on 18 March, with Lts. Bill Hardy and Ted Crosby making "five the hard way" on 6 and 26 April, respectively.

Credited with 161 victories and 12 aces from *Hornet*, Beebe's "edition" of VF-17 boosted the squadron's two-tour total to 313, narrowly edging out VF-15's single deployment record of 310.

Wartime COs:	Lt.Cdr. John T. Blackburn	1 Jan 43
	Lt.Cdr. Marshall U. Beebe	18 Apr 44

Subsequent record: redesignated VF-5B (1946), VF-61 (1948).

Disestablished 1959.

VBF-17

Established: 2 Jan 45

Deployment: *Hornet* (CV-12) Feb-Jun 45 F6F-5

Combat record: 121 victories, 8 aces. Losses unknown.
Top score: Lt(jg) John M. Johnston, 8.

The highest-scoring of all fighter-bomber squadrons was VBF-17, which split from the FitRon while at Agana, Guam, in January 1945. The next month Air Group 17 began its second wartime cruise, riding *Hornet* to Empire waters in mid-February. Operations over Japan on the 16th and 17th netted the squadron's first three victories, including one by the CO, Lt.Cdr. Hugh Nicholson. When Nicholson was killed, he was succeeded by Lt. Edwin Conant, whose true identity (John F. Perry) was only discovered in the 1950s. Perry had taken his friend's name in order to reapply for Navy flight training, and succeeded the second time—to become an ace.

VBF-17's victory log stood at 12 when the squadron tied into a flock of enemy fighters near Shikoku on 19 March. In a few minutes, 25 Japanese army and navy planes were splashed. Two days later Lt(jg) Henry Mitchell's division bagged eight, including five Bettys by Mitchell himself.

Conant's unit continued scoring in double digits: 16 kills northwest of Okinawa on 6 April; 16 more over Japan proper on the 12th; 15 on CAP two days later; and 13 over Chiran Airfield the 16th. The last confirmed victories were five Franks over Kagoshima Bay on 14 May. The deployment ended in June, with VBF-17 remaining the only fighter-bomber outfit to log more than 100 shootdowns.

Wartime COs:	Lt.Cdr. Hugh W. Nicholson +	2 Jan 45
	Lt. Edwin S. Conant	45

Subsequent record: redesignated VF-6B (1946), VF-62 (1948), VA-106 (1955). Disestablished 1969.

VF-18 (I)

Established: 20 Jul 43

Deployment: *Bunker Hill* (CV-17) Sep 43-Mar 44 F6F-3

Combat record: 74 victories, one ace. Lost 7 on deployment.
Top score: Lt.Cdr. Sam Silber, 6 (7).

Sam Silber's Fighting 18 was an ace hatchery. Though only the CO made the grade on this cruise, a dozen of his pilots (some with previous combat) were aces by war's end.

Alerted to relieve VF-17's F4Us aboard *Bunker Hill* in 1943, Silber's Hellcats filled in on short notice. They were separated from their parent air group and never did rejoin, but saw considerable combat with CAG-17. The first day of shooting was 11 November 1943 during the multi-carrier raid on Rabaul, New Britain. In an eight-hour period Silber's pilots claimed 37.5 shootdowns—nearly all Zekes and Vals—which amounted to half the victories for the entire deployment.

The tally grew to 51 by year end, largely on strength of enemy bombers snooping *Bunker Hill's* task group. Eleven more planes were shot down during January, primarily during operations against Kavieng, New Ireland. The Truk raid of 17 February netted five more kills, and another seven were logged during Marianas raids on the 22nd. Next day the last victim of the deployment—a twin-engine bomber—was downed by Lt. Bill Kelly's division. Sharing the victory was Lt. Larry Flint, who established a world's altitude record (98,500 feet) in the McDonnell F4H-1 Phantom in 1959.

Wartime CO: Lt.Cdr. Sam L. Silber 20 Jul 43

Subsequent record: No formal disestablishment. Personnel were transferred to other units by 5 Mar 44.

VF-18 (II)

Chronology: established as VGS-18 (15 Oct 42)
redesignated VC-18 (1 Mar 43), VF-36 (15 Aug 43),
VF-18 (7 Mar 44).

Deployment: *Intrepid* (CV-11) Aug-Nov 44 F6F-3, -5, -5P

Combat record: 176.5 victories, 13 aces. Lost 14 on deployment.
Top score: Lt. Cecil E. Harris, 22 (23)

With one of the fastest scoring rates in Navy history, the second VF-18 benefited from opportunities in the Formosa and Philippines campaigns. From early September to late November, the squadron rose to rank sixth highest among all Navy FitRons.

Lt.Cdr. Ed Murphy's squadron broke into combat slowly, scoring its first victory over the Philippines on 10 September 1944. Three days later eight kills were logged by six pilots, including future aces Frank Burley, Cecil Harris, Harvey Picken, and Charles Mallory. By month's end the total was 35.5, largely on the

The second VF-18 produced 13 aces during *Intrepid*'s brief 1944 deployment, including (L and R) Lt(jg) Charles Mallory and Lt. Cecil Harris. Mallory claimed 10 victories and Harris added 22 to his previous score flying F4Fs in the Solomons. FitRon 18 scored 176 victories during October and November before "Evil I" sustained kamikaze damage.

strength of 24.5 kills near Clark Field on the 21st. On that day Lt. Picken and Lt(jg) Mallory each shot down five planes during two sorties.

The next month brought unprecedented opportunity, as VF-18 claimed 121 victories during 11 days of October. One-third of those occurred on the 12th, as *Intrepid* F6Fs splashed 41 bandits over Formosa. Back in the Philippines two days later, 26 more Japanese planes fell to Fighting 18.

The record killing of 12 October was nearly matched on the 29th. During day-long sweeps over Clark Field, 38 Japanese army and navy planes—mostly fighters—were shot down. Five fell to Ens. Art Mollenhauer, who became the squadron's third ace in a day.

During November 20 more victories were recorded, including 15 on the 25th. However, that day "Evil I" was struck by *kamikazes*, prematurely ending VF-18's deployment. The squadron had shot down 176 enemy aircraft in only ten weeks, with 129 in the four days of most intense combat. Additionally, Lt. Cecil Harris became the Navy's second-ranking fighter ace with 22 victories from *Intrepid* plus one while land-based in the Solomons during 1943.

Wartime CO: Lt.Cdr. Edward J. Murphy Mar 44?

Subsequent record: redesignated VF-7A (1946), VF-71 (1948).

Disestablished 1959.

VF-19 Satan's Kittens

Established: 15 Aug 1943

Deployment: *Lexington* (CV-16) Jul-Nov 44 F6F-3, -5, -5P

Combat Record: 155 victories, 11 aces. Lost 15 on deployment.
Top score: Lt. William J. Masoner, 10 (12)

Lt.Cdr. Hugh Winters was already a combat-experienced fighter pilot when he formed VF-19 at NAAS Los Alamitos, Cal. As exec of VF-9 during the North African campaign in late 1942, he had flown F4Fs from *Ranger* (CV-4).

Deploying to Hawaii in February 1944, Satan's Kittens prepared to embark in *Lexington* that summer. Relieving VF-16 that July, Winters' unit flew its first missions against Guam that month. Subsequent combat at the Palaus and Bonins sharpened the Kittens' claws, and they were well prepared for the Philippines campaign in September.

VF-19's biggest day occurred at the height of the Battle of Leyte Gulf. On 24 October the squadron claimed 52 confirmed victories during widespread sweep, escort and CAP missions. However, there were serious losses. After Winters replaced the wounded air group commander, VF-19 had three other COs in as many weeks. The last of these, Lt. Lin Lindsay, at 25 was probably the youngest Navy squadron commander of the war.

The aces of VF-19 aboard Lexington in November 1944. Standing from left: Lt. Bruce Williams, Lt. J.J. Paskoski, Lt. Lin Lindsay, Cdr. Hugh Winters (CAG), Lt. Bus Rossi, Lt. Bill Masoner. Kneeling: Lt(jg) Al Seckel, Ens. Paul O'Mara, Lt. Jack Wheeler (ACIO), Ens. R.A. Farnsworth, and Lt(jg) Del Prater. Absent was Lt(jg) Ed Copeland, evading the Japanese with the help of Filipino guerrillas.

Following *kamikaze* damage to *Lexington* on 5 November, the air group rode "Lady Lex" to Ulithi and proceeded to the West Coast by year end. The squadron split during turnaround training at NAS Alameda, forming VBF-19 with Corsairs. Though VF-19 was the first fleet squadron with F8F-1s, the war ended before the Bearcats could taste combat.

Wartime COs:	Lt.Cdr. T. Hugh Winters	15 Aug 43
	Lt.Cdr. Franklin E. Cook +	15 Sep 44
	Lt. Roger Boles +	12 Oct 44
	Lt. Elvin L. Lindsay	5 Nov 44
	Lt.Cdr. Joseph G. Smith	Feb 45

Postwar: Redesignated VF-19A (1946) and VF-191 (1948). Disestablished NAS Miramar, Cal., 1 Mar 1978, flying F-8 Crusaders. The squadron scored one victory during the Vietnam War as Lt.Cdr. J.B. Nichols became the last naval aviator to destroy an enemy aircraft by gunfire, 9 July 1968.

VF-20

Established: 15 Oct 43

Deployment:	*Enterprise* (CV-6)	Aug-Nov 44	F6F-5, -5P
	Lexington (CV-16)	Nov 44-Jan 45	F6F-5, -5P

Combat record: 158.16 victories, 9 aces. Lost 24 plus 1 POW.
Top score: Lt(jg) Douglas Baker, 16.33.

Fighting Squadron 20 was established at NAS North Island, San Diego, on 15 October 1943. Thus began an 12-month odyssey toward combat. Embarking in *Enterprise* at the end of August 1944, Fred Bakutis' Hellcats remained aboard until 22 November when the air group transferred to *Lexington*.

The squadron's first aerial combat occurred on 11 October 1944 when Cdr. James S. Gray, previously CO of VF-6 and VF(N)-78, splashed a Betty 50 miles from the task force. By this time most dedicated night-fighter units had been absorbed into conventional VF squadrons. The next day 19 enemy fighters were downed over Formosa, four by Ens. Doug Baker, who immediately established himself as the top shooter.

Fighting 20 celebrated its first anniversary in grand style. On 15 October (16th in the U.S.), sweeps over Manila and CAPs offshore accounted for 35 shootdowns. Twenty-five pilots shared in the total, including seven future aces.

A Grumman Hellcat of VF-20, launched off CV-16, *Lexington*, in January 1945, sports the squadron's distinctive tail marking.

Top score was Ens. Walter Wood with 3.5. In the next combat, two days later, VF-20 claimed seven more victories during missions over Clark Field and Manila proper. Then on 18 October six of the eventual nine aces gained their fifth kills from a day's tally of 27.

The Battle of Leyte Gulf absorbed *Lexington's* full attention 24-26 October as CAG Dan "Dog" Smith directed strikes against enemy fleet units. Air Group 20 played a major role in sinking the battleship IJNS *Musashi* on the 24th, and though Fred Bakutis was shot down by flak, he was rescued by a submarine after a week in the water.

Back over Clark on 13 November, the squadron fought its last large combat, downing a dozen Zekes, Oscars, and Tojos, and Doug Baker ran his tally to 12.33. The next morning he bagged three Zekes and an Oscar, then disappeared. Friendly Filipinos found his body in his crashed Hellcat. Alex Vraciu, himself downed by AA that day, was given his squadronmate's dogtags.

Fighting 20's victory log was closed 21 January 1945, when a Val became the squadron's 158th victim.

Wartime COs:	Cdr. Frederick E. Bakutis	15 Oct 43
	Cdr. James S. Gray	24 Oct 44

Subsequent record: Redesignated VF-9A (1946), VF-91 (1948), VF-34 (1950), VA-34 (1955), disestablished 1969.

VF-21

Chronology: Established as VGS-11 (5 Aug 42?)
redesignated VC-11 (1 Mar 43), VF-21 (16 May 43)

Deployments:	Guadalcanal	May-Jul 43	F4F-4
	Belleau Wood (CVL-24)	Jul-Oct 44	F6F-3, -5

Combat record: 109 victories, 4 aces.
Top score: Lt. Ross E. Torkelson, 6.

Fighting 21 was typical of many "auxiliary escort squadrons" which were redesignated composite squadrons. Sent to the Solomons, VGF-11 left *Altamaha* (CVE-18) for Guadalcanal and briefly flew under its original designation. On 4 February 1943 the Wildcats claimed six Zeros on a mission to New Georgia, followed by four more while covering strikes against Japanese destroyers on the 7th. Redesignation as VC-11 came at the start of March.

The final name change occurred in mid-May, and VF-21 promptly made itself known to Cactus Fighter Command. On 30 June, covering the Rendova landings, Lt.Cdr. Whitey Ostrom's pilots claimed 30 victories, including 13 Betty bombers, losing four F4Fs. Another 27 kills were credited throughout July, the last eight Zekes being claimed the 25th. However, the squadron's only ace,

Ross Torkelson, was killed in action the 22nd.

With 69 Wildcat victories, VGF-11/VF-21 was the fourth-ranking F4F squadron of the war; second in the Navy only to VF-5.

After reforming in the U.S., the "Jack and Ace" squadron joined VT-21 (formerly VGS-12) in *Belleau Wood* during July 1944. With limited opportunities (only eight days with air-air combat) Vince Casey's pilots hunted airborne bandits over the Philippines and Formosa. First victory of the cruise was a Frances splashed on 9 September. Operations near Formosa brought four kills on 12 October and 10 more the next day, then the task force returned to the Philippines. By far the biggest day of the cruise was 15 October when VF-21 downed 18 enemy fighters in the Nichols-Nielson Field area. Four were credited to Ens. Bob Thomas, who became the only ace of the cruise. The squadron's 40th and last victory of the deployment was another Frances, splashed 18 October.

Wartime COs:	Lt.Cdr. John Hulme	15 May 43?
	Lt.Cdr. Charles H. Ostrom	25 Jun 43
	Lt.Cdr. Vincent F. Casey	27 Sep 43
	Lt.Cdr. Brainerd T. Macomber	16 Jan 45

Disestablished: 5 Nov 44

VF-22

Established: 30 Sep 42

Deployments:	*Belleau Wood* (CVL-24)	Sep 43	F6F-3
	Independence (CVL-22)	Sep-Dec 43	F6F-3
	Cowpens (CVL-25)	Jul 44-Jan 45	F6F-3, -5

Combat record: 55.83 victories, 3 aces. Lost 16 on deployment.
Top score: Lt. Clement M. Craig, 11.75

Like several of the early CVL Hellcat squadrons, VF-22 was dispersed between two ships during the summer and fall of 1943. Initially flying from *Belleau Wood*, the squadron's first kill was split with VF-24 when a Betty was splashed on 18 September. Another 5.33 victories came from *Independence* by year end. At that time the leading pilot was Lt. Clement Craig with 1.25.

Returning to combat in *Cowpens*, Craig's crew next met Japanese aircraft over the Philippines in September 1944. Two Dinahs and a Zeke were splashed on the 13th, but only four major opportunities arose thereafter. Seven bandits each were claimed over Formosa on 12 October and in Philippine waters on 15 October. Nine more splashed on the 16th, when Craig downed four Jills.

VF-22's biggest day of the war was 21 January 1945, with 16 victories. In that action off Formosa, Clem Craig bagged five Tojos while Lt(jg) Jim Bryce ran his wartime total to five, as did Ens. Ben Amsden.

Wartime COs:	Lt. Philip H. Torrey	30 Sep 42
	Lt. Leland L. Johnson	30 Sep 43
	Lt.Cdr. Thomas H. Jenkins	16 Dec 43
	Lt.Cdr. John P. Weinel	Mar 45

Disestablished: 19 Sep 45

VF-23

Established: 16 Nov 42

Deployments:	*Princeton* (CVL-23)	May 43-May 44	F6F-3
	Langley (CVL-27)	Feb-May 45	F6F-5, -5P

Combat record: 55 victories. Lost 9 pilots on deployments.
Top score: Lt(jg) L.H. Kerr, 4.83

During an uncommonly long deployment, FitRon 23 resided in *Princeton* for 12 months between May 1943 and May 1944. The last nine months were spent in combat, and the first kill was shared by Lt. Hal Funk and Lt(jg) Les Kerr 8 September 1943. A year later, leading VF-26, Funk became an FM-2 ace in a day.

A highlight of the first cruise was the Rabaul strike of 11 November, when Cdr. Hank Miller's crew claimed 10 victories. There followed three dry months before operations against the Palaus resulted in 17 kills the last two days of March 1944. Four more successes in late April brought the tally to 35.

The second deployment was in the right place at the right time, but VF-23 was able to capitalize on few opportunities. Heavy casualties dogged the unit, as Lt.Cdr. Don White was shot down and captured during the Tokyo strikes on 17 February, and two months later his successor, Merl Paddock, was KIA by flak over Japan. However, the new skipper was well experienced, as Cdr. Pug Southerland moved over from *Essex's* VF-83 and guided CVLG-23 through the rest of the cruise. Southerland had dueled Saburo Sakai over Guadalcanal on 8 August 1942. During strikes on the home islands and Okinawa, *Langley's* "kids" splashed 20 bandits, including five on 11 May.

Wartime COs:	Lt.Cdr. Henry L. Miller	16 Nov 42
	Lt.Cdr. Ralph A. Fuoss	12 May 44
	Lt.Cdr. Donald A. White +	1 Jul 44
	Lt.Cdr. Merlin Paddock +	17 Feb 45
	Cdr. James J. Southerland	21 Apr 45
	Lt. Howard L. Grimmell Jr.	15 Jul 45

Disestablished: 19 Sep 45

VF-24

Established: 31 Dec 42

Deployments:	*Belleau Wood* (CVL-24)	Sep 43-Jun 44	F6F-3
	Santee (CVE-29)	Mar-Jul 45	F6F-5, -5P

Combat record: 37.5 victories, one ace. Lost 6+ on deployments.
Top score: Lt. Robert H. Thelen, 6.5

Established the last day of 1942, VF-24 waited 21 months to fire its first shots of the war. Sharing *Belleau Wood* with part of VF-22, FitRon 24 also shared its first victory with that unit—a Betty splashed on 9 September 1943, three days after the CO, Lt.Cdr. John Curtis, was lost in an accident. Six more victories occurred during the 5 October strike against Wake Island. One of those, a Betty, fell to Lt(jg) Bob Thelen, later the squadron's lone ace.

There followed a long, frustrating semi-drought. Over the next seven months, *Belleau Wood's* Hellcats claimed only seven kills for a total 13.5 during the cruise. However, combat opportunity erupted during June 1944, beginning with a fighter sweep over Guam on the 11th. Four Japanese fighters were downed that afternoon and two more the next day. Then, on the 19th, VF-24 initiated the Turkey Shoot by splashing three Zekes over Guam at 0600. Seven more fell during the day, with Bob Thelen running his string to 6.5.

The next afternoon, during Vice Adm. Mitscher's 300-mile strike against the retreating Japanese fleet, VF-24 continued to shine. While *Belleau Wood's* Avengers sank IJNS *Hiyo*, the Hellcats claimed three more confirmed and three probables. The last kills of the cruise were logged on the 21st and 24th.

Following turnaround training, CVLG-24 became a CVEG, reporting aboard *Santee* in March 1945. VF-24's new skipper, Lt.Cdr. Rex Ostrom, was killed in action on 10 April and was succeeded by Lt. Pierre Charbonnet. The only aerial shooting of the cruise occurred on 6 April when three Jills were splashed off Okinawa. Two were credited to Ens. Roy Farmer.

Wartime COs:	Cdr. Roland H. Dale	31 Dec 42
	Lt. Cdr. John Curtis	?? 43
	Lt.Cdr. Edward M. Link, Jr.	24 Dec 43
	Lt.Cdr. Rexford J. Ostrom +	2 Sep 44
	Lt. Pierre N. Charbonnet, Jr.	10 Apr 45

Disestablished: 25 Sep 45

VF-25

Established: 15 Feb 43

Deployments:	*Cowpens* (CVL-25)	Oct 43-Jun 44	F6F-3
	Chenango (CVE-28)	Feb-Jul 45	F6F-5, -5P

Combat record: 37 victories, one ace. Lost 4+ on deployments.
Top score: Lt(jg) Donald K. McKinley, 5.

Like several early CVL FitRons, VF-25 drew first blood over Wake Island on 5 October 1943, claiming a Zeke confirmed and one probable. However, only one more victory was logged before the first Truk raid on 17 February 1944. At month's end the *Cowpens* Hellcats recorded eight shootdowns for the cruise, rising to 14 total by end of the Hollandia operation at the end of April.

When the first fighter sweep of the Marianas campaign launched on 11 June, VF-25 entered its busiest period of the war. Five Zekes and an Emily were splashed around Saipan, but the skipper was shot down while attacking a convoy near the island. He survived two weeks in the water before being rescued. Meanwhile, "Mighty Moo" Hellcats splashed four more planes through the 18th.

On 19 June, the day of the First Battle of the Philippine Sea, VF-25 claimed nine bandits in repelling a series of air attacks on Task Force 58. On that occasion Lt(jg) Don McKinley became the squadron's only ace. The 33rd victory of the cruise went into the books three days later.

Like VF-24, Fighting 25 traded a CVL's narrow deck for the shorter one of a CVE. Embarking in *Chenango* in February 1945, FitRon 25 was heavily involved in the Okinawa campaign beginning in April. Two victories were achieved that month, though skipper Richard Robinson was killed on 8 April. The final claim of the war was a Dinah on 1 June.

Wartime COs:	Lt.Cdr. Robert H. Price	6 Oct 43
	Lt.Cdr. Richard W. Robinson +	12 Sep 44
	Lt.Cdr. Paul M. Paul	5 May 45

Disestablished: 20 Sep 45

VF-26

Chronology: Established as VGF-26 (4 May 42)
Redesignated VF-26 (1 Mar 43)

Deployments:	*Sangamon* (ACV-26)	Oct 42-Jul 43	F4F-4
	Santee (CVE-29)	Apr-Oct 44	FM-2
	Fanshaw Bay (CVE-70)	Jul-Aug 45	F6F-5

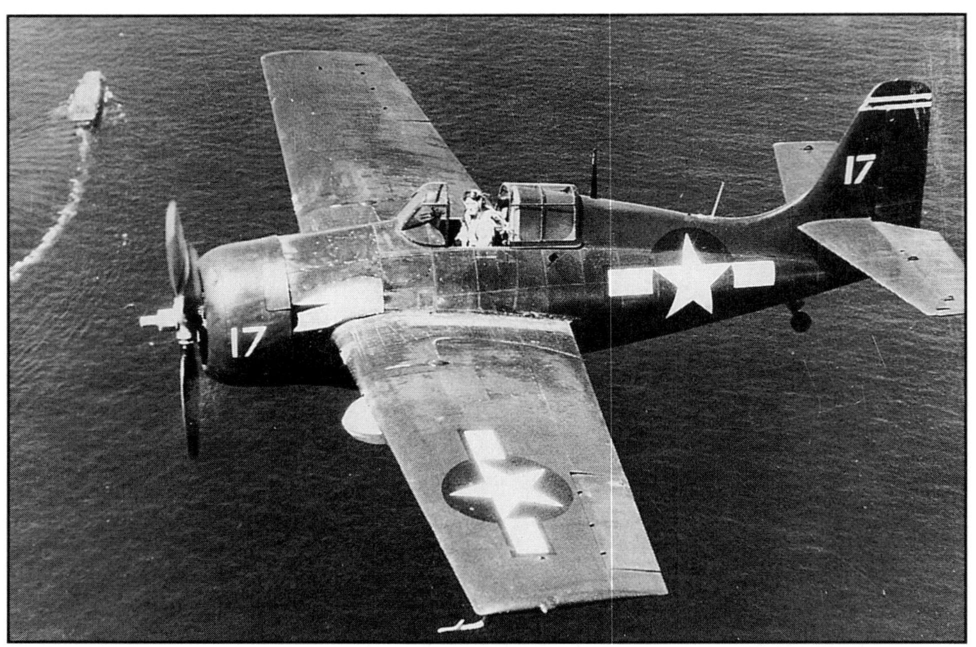

An FM-2 Wildcat of *Santee*'s VF-26 patrols off Leyte on D-Day, 20 Oct 44.

Combat record: 46 victories, one ace. Losses unknown.
Top score: Lt.Cdr. H.N. Funk, 6 (6.5)

Escort Fighting Squadron 26 went to war only five months after forming, flying in support of the invasion of North Africa during November 1942. While embarked in *Sangamon*, Lt.Cdr. W.E. Ellis' pilots claimed three French bombers and one fighter shot down on 8 November. Unlike most other CVE squadrons engaged in Torch, VGF-26 got off without serious loss.

Designated a fighter squadron in March 1943, VF-26 continued in escort carriers. Alternately flying from *Sangamon* and from land bases in the Solomons, the squadron was credited with 11 Japanese victims during June and July 1943, including eight Zekes over Kahili on 18 July.

With a dozen Axis planes to its credit, Fighting 26 began a third combat deployment in the spring of 1944. As probably the only FM-2 squadron bearing a VF label, Lt.Cdr. Harold Funk's outfit cut a swath through Japanese formations over the Philippines. In just seven days of late October the *Santee* Wildcats splashed 31 fighters and bombers during the Leyte Gulf campaign. A dozen fell on 24 October, including five by Funk, and 14 more on the 26th. The week-long spree ended the next day.

The squadron was reforming in Hawaii at war's end, and there lost the CO, Lt.Cdr. Paul Thompson, in an accident that July.

Probably no other unit flew Wildcats as long as Fighting 26: from mid-1942 until the end of 1944. At war's end VF-26 ranked sixth among Navy Wildcat units and second (31 victories) for FM-2 squadrons.

Wartime COs:	Lt.Cdr. W.E. Ellis	4 May 42
	Lt.Cdr. Harold N. Funk	15 Nov 43
	Lt.Cdr. Paul V. Thompson +	17 Jan 45
	Lt.Cdr. George R. Palus	8 Jul 45

Disestablished: 13 Nov 45

VF-27

Chronology: Established as VGF-27 (22 Apr 42)
Redesignated VF-27 (1 Mar 43)

Deployments:			
	Suwannee (ACV-27)	Oct 42-Feb, Jun 43	F4F-4
	Guadalcanal	Mar-Apr, Jul 43	F4F-4
	Princeton (CVL-23)	May-Oct 44	F6F-3, -5
	Independence (CVL-22)	Jul-Sep 45	F6F-5, -5P

Combat record: 147 victories, 10 aces. Lost 7 on deployments.
Top score: Lt. Carl A. Brown, Jr., 10.5.

Established at Norfolk in April 1942, VGF-27 became one of the most traveled Navy squadrons of the war. Following Operation Torch against French Morocco in November 1942, the squadron remained aboard *Suwannee* through most of the next eight months. Upon redesignation as VF-27 in March 1943, the squadron operated ashore at Guadalcanal until July, except for a brief period at sea in June. Among 12 victories credited during April and July were first kills for future standouts Cecil Harris and Sam Silber.

After reforming with F6Fs in the U.S., VF-27 embarked in *Princeton* for one of the most spectacular CVL cruises. Under Lt.Cdr. Ernest Wood, the sharkmouth Hellcats flew warmup missions against Saipan and Tinian 11-12 June 1944, then jumped into the Marianas Turkey Shoot. On the 19th, during four Japanese strikes against Task Force 58, VF-27 claimed 30 kills but lost Lt.Cdr. Wood, who was succeeded by Fred Bardshar. Future aces Bill Lamb, Dick Stambook, and Gordon Stanley splashed four raiders apiece.

Bardshar took a large fighter sweep to Manila on 21 September, leading VF-27 to 38 victories over Japanese army and navy fighters. It was the squadron's biggest haul of the war, as Lt. John Rodgers claimed a heartbreaking 4.5 kills on the only day he scored. Lt. Jim Shirley, en route to acedom, gained four more.

After Formosa strikes in mid-October, *Princeton* was back in Leyte Gulf on the 24th. Near Pollilo Island in the gulf, FitRon 27 played merry hell with enemy fighters, destroying 36. Four pilots emerged as aces in a day: Lts. Carl Brown and Jim Shirley plus Lt(jg) Gene Townsend and Ens. Tom Conroy. However, upon return to the task force, "Sweet P" was afire and sinking from a conventional air attack.

One of VF-27s colorfully marked Hellcats finds refuge aboard a stranger 24 Oct 44. In the background her home base, the mortally wounded CVL-23, *Princeton*, can be seen burning furiously.

Air Group 27's cruise was over. Of the 134 victories credited during the deployment, a staggering 104 occurred on three days.

Bardshar reformed the squadron in time to return to WestPac in *Independence*. One more victory was scored before the war ended.

Wartime COs:	Lt.Cdr. T.K. Wright	42
	Lt. J.T. Fitzpatrick, Jr. +	Jan 43
	Lt.Cdr. J. Roudebush	15 Oct 43
	Lt.Cdr. Ernest W. Wood +	26 Dec 43
	Lt.Cdr. Frederick A. Bardshar	19 Jun 44

Disestablished: 26 Oct 45

VF-28

Chronology: Established as VGF-28 (1 May 42)
Redesignated VF-28 (1 Mar 43)

Deployments:			
	Suwannee (ACV-27)	Nov 42	F4F-4
	Guadalcanal	Apr-Jul 42	F4F-4
	Chenango (CVE-28)	Jun-Jul 43	F4F-4
	Monterey (CVL-26)	May-Dec 44	F6F-3, -5

Combat record: 67 victories, 2 aces. Lost 4+ pilots deployed.
Top scores: Lts. Oscar C. Bailey and D.C. Clements, 5 each.

VGF-28 shared *Suwannee* with three other squadrons during Operation Torch for a total complement of 29 F4Fs and nine TBFs. However, no aerial combat was offered the Fighting 28 Wildcats, who had to await their chance at the war in the Pacific for air-to-air gunnery. Alternately flying from Guadalcanal, the Russells, and *Chenango*, VF-28 (redesignated 1 March 1943) claimed two Zekes in April and 10 during July. Top scorers were Lt(jg)s J.H. Waring with four Zekes and Roy Reed with two.

Ten months later, equipped with Hellcats, VF-28 deployed in *Monterey* under the guidance of Lt.Cdr. Roger Mehle, a VF-6 alumnus. The skipper showed his new guys how it was done, claiming two Zekes and two probables over Tinian on 11 June 1944. Nineteen kills were credited on the day of the Turkey Shoot, 19 June, when Mehle splashed two Jills. He thereby ran his wartime total to 5.66, while Lts. Buck Bailey claimed four Zekes and Don Clements three.

Only three more victories were credited until the Philippine campaign heated up in mid-October. VF-28 splashed three snoopers from the 12th to the 14th, then bagged 10 bombers and fighters on the 15th. The second-best day of the cruise was 5 November when 14 assorted army and navy types were downed in the Clark Field area with Ens. R.L. Richardson claiming three.

The squadron's final two victories of the war occurred on 11 November and 14 December, raising the tally to 67.

Wartime COs:		
	Lt.Cdr. J.I. Bandy	1 May 42
	Lt.Cdr. Richard C. Merrick	22 Oct 43
	Lt.Cdr. Roger W. Mehle	6 Mar 44
	Lt.Cdr. Maynard M. Furney	8 Mar 45

Disestablished: 6 Nov 45

VF-29

Chronology: Established as VGF-29 (18 Jul 42)
Redesignated VF-29 (1 Mar 43)

Deployment:	*Santee* (ACV-29)	Oct 42-Dec 43	F4F-4
	Cabot (CVL-28)	Oct 44-Apr 45	F6F-5, -5P

Combat record: 114 victories, 12 aces. Lost 7 on deployments.
Top score: Lt(jg) Robert E. Murray, 10.33

For one of the more distinguished "smallboy" squadrons of the war, Fighting 29 got off to a poor start. With 14 Wildcats embarked in *Santee* during four days of Operation Torch, the squadron lost 10 aircraft and one pilot killed plus four others briefly captured by the Vichy French. The skipper, Tom Blackburn, ditched at sea on 8 November and remained in the water until late on the 10th. Two months later he established VF-17 with F4Us.

The squadron's only victory of Torch came on 10 November when Ens. Bruce Jaques splashed a Potez 63 reconnaissance bomber.

An F6F Hellcat of VF-29 lands a bit long aboard CVL-28, *Cabot,* on 13 Feb 45.

Following departure from *Santee* a year later, VF-29 reformed as part of Air Group 29 in *Cabot*. Under Lt.Cdr. Bill Eder, a veteran of VF-2 and -3 during early 1942, the squadron demonstrated its competence in a two-ocean war. On 10 October 1944 the first Japanese victims fell to now-Lt. Bruce Jaques and his wingman, who bagged a pair of Frans off Formosa. Thus, Jaques scored VF-29's first three kills against two Axis nations.

As if making up for so few previous opportunities in two years, aerial targets appeared in profusion that month. On 16 October the squadron defended two U.S. cruisers that had been torpedoed off Formosa and, in barely two hours, claimed 34 kills. Two pilots became instant aces as Lt. Al Fecke and Ens. Bob Buchanan destroyed five planes apiece. By month's end, VF-29's Pacific Theater tally stood at 63, with 10 more added by New Year's.

The Home Island strikes on 16-17 February resulted in eight more shootdowns, plus five more during a "return engagement" a week later. Sweeps and strikes over Omura Airfield on 18 March brought 10 more victories, and making an ace of Bill Eder, who first had fired his guns in defense of the old *Lexington* off Rabaul 37 months before. The last sixteen victories occurred near Okinawa in the first week of April, ranking VF-29 as one of the top 20 Hellcat squadrons of the war.

Wartime COs:	Lt.Cdr. John T. Blackburn	18 Jul 42
	Lt. Harry B. Bass	21 Dec 42
	Lt.Cdr. Willard E. Eder	10 Apr 44
	Lt.Cdr. John J. Hilton	10 Jun 45

Disestablished: 10 Sep 45

VF-30

Established: 1 Apr 43

Deployments:	*Monterey* (CVL-26)	Nov 43-May 44	F6F-3
	Belleau Wood (CVL-24)	Jan-Jun 45	F6F-5, -5P

Combat record: 159.83 victories, 10 aces. Lost 17 on deployments.
Top score: Ens. James V. Reber, 11.

Fighting 30 got off to a fast start, scoring its first kill 19 November 1943, nine days after boarding *Monterey*. Following the Tarawa operation, three more Bettys were splashed by year end, including one shared with VF-18 on Christmas Day.

Thirteen more planes, including two bombers, fell to Fighting 30 near Kavieng, New Ireland, on New Year's Day 1944. Subsequent ops at Truk Atoll and the Marianas added another seven though the end of February. Then, during the last two days of March the squadron engaged in hard-fought combat over the Palaus. Six fighters were claimed on the 30th and 18.33 the 31st. The cruise's final claims came a month later, with two Zekes on 30 April. They raised the tally to 49.33, paced by Lt(jg) E.A. Evenson's 6.25. Two others who made ace on the cruise were Hank Carey (four plus three previous) and George Formanek (two plus three prior), the latter being killed while strafing over New Guinea 23 April.

Returning to the Pacific in January 1945, VF-30 found good hunting aboard *Belleau Wood*. Lt.Cdr. Robert Lindner's squadron went against Tokyo on 16 February, claiming four kills that day but the CAG was killed near Iwo Jima on the 23rd. He was succeeded by Lt.Cdr. Doug Clark, who oversaw six more victories by 19 March. On the 21st two divisions splashed 21 bandits on ForceCAP, providing a warmup for the main event of 6 April, the Navy's fourth-highest scoring day of the war.

During two hours of *kamikaze* action, VF-30 claimed a stunning 47 victories. Sixteen were credited to the last CVL aces in a day: Ensigns Carl Foster, Ken Dahms and Johnnie Miller.

The squadron continued depleting the suiciders with 15 shootdowns on 12 April and 13 more by month's end. FitRon 30's final victories of the war were a Frank and Betty on 25 May, the last one becoming the skipper's second. The cruise's tally of 110 victories brought the wartime total to 159.33.

Wartime COs:	Lt.Cdr. James G. Sliney	1 Apr 43
	Lt.Cdr. Robert H. Lindner +	25 Jun 44
	Lt.Cdr. Douglas A. Clark	23 Feb 45

Disestablished: 10 Sep 45

VF-31 Flying Meataxers

Established: 1 May 43

Deployments:	*Cabot* (CVL-28)	Jan-Sep 44	F6F-3
	Belleau Wood (CVL-24)	Jul-Sep 45	F6F-5, -5P

Combat record: 165.6 victories, 14 aces. Losses unknown.
Top score: Lt(jg) Cornelius N. Nooy, 19.

VF-31 proved that Independence-class FitRons, with half the planes and pilots, could capitalize upon their opportunities and equal or even outscore some Essex-class fighters. On 29 January 1944, Lt.Cdr. Bob Winston led his *Cabot* squadron over Roi Island and splashed the first of five Zekes to begin a nine-month string. The next combat, 30 April, launched the string of Lt(jg) Connie Nooy, who claimed a triple.

The first fighter sweep over Tinian on 11 June inaugurated the Marianas campaign, with the Meataxers claiming 14 kills. They doubled that figure eight

F6F-3 in VF-31 markings at the National Museum of Naval Aviation in Pensacola, Florida. The Hellcat bears the personal markings of Lt(jg) Ray Hawkins, one of the "Meataxers" top aces.

days later, at the height of the Turkey Shoot, as Lt(jg) John Wirth splashed four raiders and four others claimed three each.

Winston's crew observed the Fourth of July over Iwo Jima, as Nooy splashed four and Lt. Al Mencin added three of 13 kills. September brought the two biggest days of the cruise: 25 victories the morning of the 13th in combats over Negros and Luzon, with Lt(jg) Ray Hawkins becoming an ace in a day. Then, on the 21st, the Meataxers visited Manila and environs, leaving 29 enemy fighters in the dirt. Five were credited to Nooy. The cruise's shooting ended the next day when six Vals were downed south of Lingayen. It brought the squadron total to 146.6 victories. *Winston*, who had written a book about Navy flying before the war, later described the *Cabot* cruise in *Fighting Squadron*.

Winston was relieved by Lt.Cdr. Danny Wallace, who was killed in a night flying accident in March 1945. His successor was Bruce Weber, who had led VF-34 in the Solomons.

The second cruise, beginning aboard *Belleau Wood* in July 1945, produced only three days of air combat. Eight bandits were claimed over Yokaichi Airfield on the 25th, including Connie Nooy's last four. Four more succumbed on the 18th. Fighting 31 splashed seven bandits on 15 August, including Ens. Clarence Moore's Judy, the last kill of the war. These 19 kills raised the total to 165.60, highest for any CVL FitRon.

Wartime COs:	Lt.Cdr. Robert A. Winston	1 May 43
	Lt.Cdr. Daniel J. Wallace, Jr. +	Sep 44
	Lt.Cdr. Bruce S. Weber	14 Mar 45

Disestablished: 25 Oct 45

VF-32 Outlaw's Bandits

Established: 1 Jun 43

Deployments:	*Langley* (CVL-27)	Jan-Oct 44	F6F-3/5
	Cabot (CVL-28)	Aug-Sep 45	F6F-5

Combat record: 44 victories, 2 aces. Lost 3 on deployments.
Top score: Lt.Cdr. Eddie C. Outlaw, 6.

Established at NAS Willow Grove in June 1943, VF-32 was led by Lt.Cdr. Eddie Outlaw, from the Annapolis class of '35. The squadron deployed to combat only six months later, embarked in *Langley*. The first victory went to Lt(jg) Dick May, who splashed a Betty off the Palaus on 29 March 1944. It was the first of only nine days of aerial combat logged by "Outlaw's Bandits" during almost ten months in the Pacific.

During the second Truk raid, 29 April, VF-32 accounted for half its wartime tally in a frantic combat. Outlaw gunned five of 21 claimed Zekes to become the squadron's first ace and the first CVL ace in a day. Meanwhile, Lt(jg) Don Reeves claimed four and Dick May three. Lt. Holly Hills, previously an RCAF Mustang pilot, also scored a triple.

The leadoff sweep over Saipan on 11 June added six more victories to the Bandits' log, but the rest of the Marianas campaign proved disappointing, with just three more kills.

However, more opposition arose during 21 September missions against Manila. VF-32 dropped 11 more "meatballs," with May and Hills becoming aces. Hills technically was not a Navy ace, but his fourth Japanese plane was his fifth of the war. He had claimed the Mustang's first victory with a FW-190 over Dieppe in August 1942.

The Bandits' scoring ended the next day when a Sally and Oscar were destroyed in two different missions. In all, 21 pilots contributed to the total of 44 victories.

When Japan surrendered in August 1945, VF-32 was aboard *Cabot*, but flew only one mission before the end of hostilities.

Wartime COs:	Lt.Cdr. Eddie C. Outlaw	1 Jun 43
	Lt.Cdr. George N. Eisenhart	24 Aug 44
	Lt. Leon T. Raynor	22 Aug 45

Disestablished: 13 Nov 45

VF-33

Chronology: Established as VGS-16 (8 Aug 42)
Redesignated VC-16 (1 Mar 43), VF-33 (15 Aug 43).

Deployments:			
	Guadalcanal	Aug-Sep 43	F6F-3
	New Georgia	Oct-Jan 44	F6F-3
	Sangamon (CVE-26)	Feb-May 45	F6F-5, -5P
	Chenango (CVE-28)	Jul-Sep 45	F6F-5, -5P

Combat record: 90.5 victories, 3 aces. Lost 12 pilots.
Top score: Ens. Frank E. Schneider 7

Upon establishment at Seattle in August 1942, VGS-16 shared the careers of many other escort scouting squadrons, finally being designated a FitRon on 15 August 1943. Flying F6F-3s, Lt. Cdr. Monk Russell's outfit arrived at Guadalcanal the 27th of that month. Ens. Jim Warren claimed the first kill, a Zeke over Margusial Island on 6 September. By month's end VF-33 was credited with 20 victories, including three by Lt. Ken Hildebrandt over Ballali on the 14th.

Moving northward to Segi Point, New Georgia, on 19 October, the squadron was better positioned to support strikes in the upper Solomons. The next day four more fighters were splashed east of Kahili.

Over Empress Augusta Bay on 8 November, Lt(jg) J.J. Kinsella claimed three planes to become an ace. His first two dated from VF-72 nine months before. The second Rabaul strike on 11 November resulted in 5.5 more victories for the squadron.

A VF-33 F6F-5E on *Sangamon*'s port catapult in early 1945. First entering combat as a land-based Hellcat squadron in the Solomons during 1943, FitRon 33 produced some of the earliest F6F aces.

Fifteen kills were registered in December, including six on Christmas Eve, the day Ken Hildebrandt scored his fifth. Missions against Rabaul continued into January, with a dozen claims in the first nine days of the month. Ens. Frank Schneider ran his string to six with a double on the 2nd, followed by another on the 9th. That same day Ens. Jack Watson claimed his fourth.

Among the earliest F6F squadrons in combat, VF-33 led all land-based Hellcat units with 74.5 victories.

A split tour began aboard *Sangamon* in February 1945, beginning operations off Okinawa in late March. First victory of the cruise was a Val on the 26th, with 15 subsequuent splashes through April. Nine of those occurred over Myako Jima on the 22nd, with an Oscar becoming Jack Watson's fifth of the war. On the last day of the month a Tony became VF-33's 90th shootdown. The subsequent time in*Chenango,* July to September, produced no further opportunity.

Wartime COs:	Lt.Cdr. Hawley A. Russell	43
	Lt.Cdr. Paul C. Rooney	20 Apr 44

Disestablished: 19 Nov 45

VF-34 (I)

Chronology: Established as VGS-34 (24 Feb 43)
Redesignated VC-34 (1 Mar 43), VF-34 (15 Aug 43)

Deployment: Solomon Islands Mar-May 44 F6F-3

Combat record: No victories. Lost 5 pilots while deployed.

Fighting 34 was, like many squadrons of its origin, independent of any air group. Designated a FitRon in August 1943, it received 16 Hellcats when its skipper, Lt.Cdr. Bruce Weber, reported aboard 24 September. During training at Brown Field, San Diego, VF-34 become known as the "braid squadron" owing to its many senior lieutenants who had been flight instructors.

Upon leaving NAS North Island on board seaplane tender *Kokomo*, VF-34 arrived in Hawaii and moved to MCAS Ewa. Subsequently the squadron was ferried to Espiritu Santo in Marine Corps R5Cs, where it picked up VF-33's old F6Fs.

After staging through New Georgia and Green Island, Bruce Weber's pilots succeeded VF-17 on Bougainville in early March 1944. By that time the hunting had thinned out, and Fighting 34 seldom saw an airborne Japanese aircraft. The Hellcats did, however, strafe barges, trucks, and other targets of opportunity.

In May 1944 FitRon 34 embarked in the CVE *Marcus Island*, sailing from the Russells to the West Coast. The squadron stood down in early July, with personnel redistributed to other units.

Bruce Weber went on to command VF-98, the fighter RAG at Los Alamitos, then led Air Group 31. Another alumnus, Lt. Paul Pugh, finally logged air-to-air combat in Korea. As an F-86 exchange pilot in the 4th Fighter Wing he downed two MiG-15s—and was recalled to Far East Air Force HQ until Capt. Jim Jabara notched Number Five.

Wartime CO: Lt.Cdr. Bruce Weber 24 Sep 43

Disestablished: 8 Jul 44

VF-34 (II)

Chronology: Established as VF-48 (Jun 44)
Redesignated VF-53 (2 Jan 45)
Redesignated VF-34 (1 Apr 45)

Deployment: *Monterey* (CVL-26) Apr-Sep 45 F6F-5, -5P

Combat record: 3.5 victories. Lost 2 pilots on deployment.
Top score: Lt. Oscar M. Rupert, 2.

When VF-53 was forced off the *kamikaze*-stricken *Saratoga* in February 1945, portions of the squadron reformed as a new VF-34. Quickly reshuffled and attached to *Monterey*, the squadron had to adapt to new living conditions, trading in the largest carrier afloat for a CVL's narrow deck.

Aerial combat presented itself only two days of VF-34's existence. On the morning of 14 May Lt(jg) Homer Savage shared a Zeke with VF-47—apparently overhead the task force. Later that morning Lt. Oscar Rupert splashed a Hamp and Lt. Bill Bertram a Dinah.

There followed three months without aerial combat, but on 13 August Rupert caught a Frank and destroyed it, raising the squadron tally to 3.5 confirmed. Hostilities ended two days later.

Wartime CO: Lt.Cdr. Robert W. Conrad Jun 44

Disestablished: 8 Jul 45

VF-35

Chronology: Established as VGS-35 (28 Jan 43)
Redesignated VC-35 (1 Mar 43)
Redesignated VF-35 (15 Jul 43)

Deployment: *Chenango* (CVE-28) Oct 43-Nov 44 F6F-3/5

Combat record: 9 victories. Lost 4 pilots on deployment.
Top score: Lt. Samuel W. Forrer, 2.5

Fighting 35 derived from VC-35 at San Diego in July 1943 and deployed to the Pacific only four months later. In one of the longest continuous assignments of WW II, VF-35 spent 13 months aboard *Chenango*, but waited eight months to draw first blood. Lt(jg) H.E. Magnusson's division splashed a Betty on 21 June, and Lt(jg) W.F. Cyrus' team destroyed another the next day.

Nearly four months later, on 18 October, VF-35 began the most active period of its career. Lt. Sam Forrer and his wingman bagged a Fran off Mindanao, plus a Sally by himself 25 hours later. The squadron added three more victories from the 20th to the 23rd, then closed its account with a two fighters destroyed on the 28th. The last fell to Forrer, who bagged an Oscar over Leyte to emerge as top shooter for the deployment.

The nine victories were shared by 11 pilots.

Wartime COs:	Lt.Cdr. S. Mandarich	15 Jul 43
	Lt.Cdr. Frederick T. Moore	15 Mar 44
	Lt. Edward W. Simpson, Jr.	7 Jan 45

Disestablished: 19 Nov 45

VF-37

Established: 15 Jul 43

Deployment: *Sangamon* (CVE-26) Nov 43-Oct 44 F6F-3/5

Combat record: 20 victories. Losses unknown.
Top score: Lt(jg) Karl W. Kenyon, 4.

Second most successful among the CVE F6F squadrons was VF-37, which scored all but one of its 20 victories during the Battle of Leyte Gulf. Embarking in *Sangamon* in November 1943, Lt.Cdr. Stan Hindman's troops spent nearly a full year awaiting their big chance. The only break in the monotony occurred during the Marianas campaign when Lt(jg) Warren Boemers splashed a Judy on 22 June 1944.

However, on 24 October the *Sangamon* Hellcats found their chance over Leyte and Tacloban Island. Intercepting two batches of enemy aircraft, Fighting 37 splashed nine. In one of the war's least-acclaimed fighter actions, Lt(jg) Karl Kenyon made nine claims: four Sallys destroyed, three probables and two damaged!

The next morning five planes were downed over Leyte as the CO's division tangled with Zekes. That afternoon a Jill also was destroyed.

On the 26th two Oscars were credited destroyed with two damaged. Then, in two actions the 27th, three more Japanese fighters were engaged. Two were destroyed while the last, a Zeke, was credited to Hindman as a probable. In all, 11 pilots contributed to the total 20 victories.

Wartime COs:	Lt.Cdr. F.L. Bates	15 Jul 43
	Lt.Cdr. Stanley E. Hindman	23 May 44

Disestablished: 20 Dec 45

VF-38

Established: 22 Jun 43

Deployments: Solomon Islands Sep 43 - Mar 44 F6F-3

Combat record: 22 victories. Losses unknown.
Top score: Lt(jg) Wilson C. Kelly, 4.5

Ranking second among land-based Navy Hellcat squadrons, VF-38 fought the Solomons campaign from September 1943 to March 1944. Operating from Guadalcanal, the first claim was a Zeke probable north of Ballale Island on 14 September, with Lt. Oscar "Oc" Chenoweth gaining the first kill in the same area the next day. Shortly he left the squadron to join VF-17, where he became a Corsair ace. Lt(jg) Wilson Kelly, later VF-38's top scorer, also opened his account on the 15th. Ballale continued with good hunting when four Zekes were claimed the 16th.

Moving to Segi Point, New Georgia, VF-38 had just set up camp when Lt(jg) Cliff Gartell bagged a Zeke on the 21st. The squadron remained at Segi until 10 December, then relocated north to Bougainville in late January.

Operating from Barakoma and the Piva Yoke strips, the Hellcats claimed six confirmed between the 21st and 31st, mainly over New Britain. As the pressure on Rabaul increased, so did combat opportunities. Ten kills were confirmed from six combats from 5 to 19 February, with five more claimed as probables. In the last air-air combat, the 19th, VF-38 scored five kills, two probables and four damaged.

Wilson Kelly came achingly close to acedom, with 4.5 victories, followed by five more pilots with multiple kills.

Wartime COs:	Lt.Cdr. John H. Anderson ?	43
	Lt.Cdr. Alfred I. Boyd, Jr.	21 May 44
	Lt.Cdr. Charles D. Fonvielle, Jr.	15 Feb 45

Disestablished: 31 Jan 46

VF-39 (I)

Chronology: Established as VC-64 (1 Jun 43)
Redesignated VF-39 (15 Aug 43)

Deployment: Majuro Atoll Feb-Jun 44 F6F-3

Combat record: No victories. Lost 5 officers.

Composite Squadron 64 was established at NAS Seattle in June 1943 but quickly lost its identity. FitRon 39 was formed as a stand-alone unit without a parent air group, specifically for land-based operations in the Central Pacific.

From February to June 1944, the squadron was based at Majuro Atoll in the Marshall Islands. Thus, while the fast carriers were engaged from Truk to the Marianas, VF-39 languished in the backwater of the war, flying routine searches and patrols to bypassed islands such as Wotje and Mille.

Fighting 39 was only the second FitRon (after the first VF-34) to complete a tour without aerial victory claims. During 1945, two other day squadrons (VF-87 and VBF-94) similarly were unable to engage Japanese planes in the air.

A second VF-39 was established at Atlantic City in March 1945 and stood down without seeing action.

Wartime CO: unknown

Disestablished: 15 Jul 44

VF-40 Flying Boars

Chronology: Established as VC-20 (1 Jul 42)
Redesignated VF-40 (15 Jun 43)

Deployment:	Solomons	Sep 43-Mar 44	F6F-3
	Suwannee (CVE-27)	Feb-Sep 45	F6F-5

Combat record: 29 victories, one ace. Lost 7 plus 1 POW.
Top score: Ens. Robert B. Carlson, 5.

Formed at El Centro, California, from VC-20's fighters, VF-40 wasted little time getting into the war. Three months after designation as a FitRon, the squadron arrived at Guadalcanal. Lt. Alex Brittain claimed a Zeke on 14 September, the second day ashore, and pilots added two more on a return mission to Ballale the 15th.

Cdr. John Rembert's F6Fs next operated from Segi Point on New Georgia 17 October to 13 November but moved to Barakoma, Vella Lavella, on 11 December. Combats in this period accounted for one probable and six damaged over New Ireland. The new year rang in with two Zekes confirmed and two probables, and Rabaul strikes brought 14 more victories during the month. One of two Zekes bagged near Rapopo Airfield, Rabaul, on 23 January raised Ens. Bob Carlson's score to five.

On 24 February Fighting 40 advanced to Bougainville, finally concluding its tour in the Treasury Islands 19 March. No further victories were claimed, however, resulting in a tie for second-highest Hellcat land-based squadron: 20 kills each for VF-38 and -40.

Almost a year later—in February 1945—VF-40 returned to combat, now aboard *Suwannee*. The nine shootdowns of the cruise were all related to the Okinawa campaign, where Lt.Cdr. Richard Sampson was killed on 5 April. His successor, Lt.Cdr. Jim Longino, led off with a Myrt on the 12th. He and two other pilots splashed five Sonias the next day, but a full month passed without further claims. Then, on 15 May, Ens. Ray Lebel and Lt(jg) Joe Coleman combined on three Vals, bringing the squadron total to 29.

Wartime COs:	Lt.Cdr. John P. Rembert	1 Jul 42
	Lt.Cdr. Richard D. Sampson +	1 Jun 44
	Lt.Cdr. James C. Longino, Jr.	5 Apr 45

Disestablished: 19 Nov 45

A Grumman Hellcat of VF-40 leaves *Suwanee*, CVE-27, in 1945.

VF-41 Red Rippers

See VF-4 entry

The Red Rippers enjoyed one of the longest careers in Navy history. Established as VF-5 in 1927, they became VF-4 in 1937 and were redesignated VF-41 in 1941. The Rippers reverted to Fighting Four in August 1943 and survived to fly F-14 Tomcats into the 1990s. This F4F-3, with lightweight bombs beneath the wings, prepares to launch from Ranger in the last days of peace—3 December 1941. (credit Tailhook Assn.)

VF(N)-41

Chronology: Established as VF(N)-79 (20 Jan 44)
Redesignated VF(N)-41 (25 Aug 44)

Deployment: *Independence* (CVL-22) Aug 44-Jan 45 F6F-5N

Combat record: 46 victories, 2 aces. Lost 7 pilots deployed.
Top score: Lt. William E. Henry, 9.5

Though other night fighter units had deployed in carriers, none operated as a full squadron until Cdr. Turner Caldwell took VF(N)-41 aboard *Independence* in August 1944. Wearing two hats as VF skipper and CAG, the former SBD pilot was determined to succeed in what had been called "an experiment in suicide."

Despite the Night Hellcats' capability, task group commanders were reluctant to make full use of the potential. Consequently, the first ten kills were made in daylight, beginning 12 September when Ensigns George Obenour and Bob Klock bagged a Betty that morning. In the evening Lt. Bill Henry and Ens. Jack Berkheimer combined to splash a Dinah. Both would add to their scores.

The first pure night kills were scored the evening of 12 October when three Bettys were downed near the task group, two by Bill Henry. Three Emilys went down the next night in Formosan waters, as Jack Berkheimer scored a double and tied Henry at 4.50. Henry then splashed another Emily at 0300 on the 15th to become the squadron's first ace.

Four additional kills were claimed the morning of the 24th, including a pair by Berkheimer. *Independence* Hellcats and Avengers tracked the Japanese center force through Surigao Strait that night, providing crucial information to Adm. Halsey's staff.

Remaining in the Philippines, the squadron logged nine more kills during two weeks of November, including five at night. Three more consecutive nights of action occurred in mid-December, with kills on the 14th, 15th and 16th. However, on the 14th Berkheimer disappeared chasing a nocturnal bogey overland and was never seen again. He was thought to have collided with a Japanese aircraft he was trying to intercept.

A record six victories were scored on 6 January 1945, with Ens. Emmett Edwards accounting for half of those over Luzon. The squadron claimed three more on the 10th, then closed its victory log with Bill Henry's tenth, an Oscar southwest of Canton, China, on the 16th.

Of 46 credited victories, about 20 were claimed at night.

Wartime CO: Cdr. Turner F. Caldwell 20 Jan 44

Disestablished: 25 Feb 46

"Cupid 5," an F6F-5N of VF(N)-41 ready to launch from *Independence* in Formosan waters during October 1944. As part of the first carrier-based night air group committed to combat, FitRon 41 flew from the CVL from August 1944 into January 1945, claiming 46 shootdowns, including at least 20 at night.

VF-42 (I)

Chronology: Established as VS-1B (May 1928)
Redesignated VS-1S (1930), VS-1B (1931), VS-41 (1937), VF-42 (1941)

Deployment: *Yorktown* (CV-5) Dec 41-May 42 F4F-3

Combat record: 25 victories. Lost 5 officers, 1 enlisted.
Top score: Lt(jg) Arthur J. Brassfield, 4.33

Among the unheralded Navy squadrons of all time, Fighting 42 earned a place of honor which many famous units might envy.

Redesignated a FitRon from Scouting 41 on 15 March 1941, Lt. Pete Pedersen's outfit was originally a *Ranger* unit which converted from SBU biplane scout bombers to F4F-3s that same year. At the time of Pearl Harbor the squadron was embarked in *Yorktown*, spelling VF-5 which had only recently transitioned from F3Fs to Wildcats. With no time to shake out, Fighting Five remained on the East Coast while VF-42 rode *Yorktown* to the Pacific.

Fighting 42 was loaded with talent. Under Lt.Cdrs. Charlie Fenton (CO) and Jim Flatley (XO), the squadron boasted standouts and/or future aces including Art Brassfield, Dick Crommelin, Walt Haas, Bill Leonard, and Scott McCuskey.

A series of hit-and-run raids in the Central and South Pacific kept "Old Yorky" on the move in early 1942. The Navy's fourth fighter victory of the war was scored by VF-42 on 1 February during a raid in the Gilberts. A subsequent attack on Tulagi netted three more splashes, just before the two-day Battle of the Coral Sea.

Fighting 42 performed splendidly on 7 and 8 May, first during the strike which sank light carrier *Shoho*, then in defense of the task force. Again on the 8th, strike escort and CAP resulted in heavy combat which raised the squadron tally to 25 victories.

Most of Fenton's pilots remained aboard when the CO departed for reassignment and Flatley went to the US to form VF-10. Days later, operating under Jimmy Thach, the resident Yorktowners accounted for eighteen of Fighting Three's 33 victories at Midway.

A second VF-42 was established 19 July 1945, far too late to reach combat.

Wartime COs:	Lt.Cdr. Oscar Pedersen	15 Mar 41
	Lt.Cdr. Charles R. Fenton	Apr 42

Disestablished: 22 Jun 42

VF-44 Crusaders

Established: 1 Feb 44

Deployment: *Langley* (CVL-27) Oct 44-Feb 45 F6F-5, -5P

Combat record: 47 victories, 3 aces. Lost 10 on deployment.
Top score: Cdr. Malcolm T. Wordell, 7.

Fighting 44 benefited from a battle-wise skipper. Mac Wordell had been exec of VF-41 during Operation Torch, and was known as an officer who took care of his troops. Like most CVL fighter COs, Wordell doubled as CAG. Thus, when *Langley* sailed that fall of 1944, the air group was ready, with a few Torch veterans to lend experience.

Beginning 13 October, FitRon 44 splashed four snoopers in five days as the Philippine campaign got underway.

More than half the squadron's victories were claimed 24 October, when two dozen Japanese planes fell to VF-44 CAPs. That morning John Montapert splashed three Zekes and a Kate to become the first ace. Mac Wordell notched a Tony, then chased down the Judy which bombed and sank *Princeton*. Lt. Carl Brunmier and Ens. Milo Shaffer each scored triples during the day.

Four more victories came over Leyte and Luzon on the 27th, ending the month with a total 32 victories.

The next three kills came on 5-6 November, with Carl Brunmier achieving acedom with a pair of Zekes. The squadron added five more victories the 11th, dropping assorted Japanese fighters into Ormoc Bay. The skipper notched three Tonys to make ace himself, almost exactly three years after he was downed by AA over Morocco. His sixth victory, a Dinah, splashed on the 25th.

CVL-27, *Langley*, heels over in heavy weather in the So. China Sea as crew maintenance men and Hellcats of VF-44 ride out a typhoon.

Lt. Chuck August, another Torch veteran, shared a Jake with his wingman on 15 December to conclude scoring for the year. John Montapert logged his sixth kill on 3 January, one of two successes that day. Then Mac Wordell closed VF-44's victory log when he bagged a Betty off the Formosa coast on 21 January. In all, 22 pilots contributed to the squadron's 47 victories.

Wartime CO: Cdr. Malcolm T. Wordell 1 Feb 44
Cdr. Stanley W. Vejtasa 11 Jun 45

Disestablished: 15 Sep 45

VF-45

Established: 1 Apr 44

Deployment: *San Jacinto* (CVL-30) Nov 44-May 45 F6F-5

Combat record: 81.5 victories, 6 aces. Lost 7 on deployment.
Top score: Lt. James B. Cain, 8.

Arriving in WestPac in November 1944, Fighting 45 logged most of its combat over Okinawa and the Japanese home islands. Initial air combat occurred 3 January 1945 when the CO, Cdr. Gordon Schecter, led a division which

A Hellcat fighter of VF-45 takes a wave-off from the LSO of *San Jacinto*.

claimed a Nick probably destroyed near Kobe. The first two confirmed kills were recorded on ForceCAP the 21st.

During the Tokyo strike on 16 February, VF-45 led all CVL FitRons with 28 shootdowns. Gordon Schecter and Lt(jg) L.H. Kidwell both scored five victories during the day as *Langley* Hellcats fought a half-dozen enemy aircraft types. Lt. Jim Cain, later the top scorer, began his string with 2.5 kills.

A half-dozen victories were made in three days of March, all Jills snooping the task group. However, Schecter was killed by AA guns over Okinawa on the 18th.

The *kamikaze* surge of 6 and 16 April brought repeated opportunities for the CVL squadrons, which typically drew more CAPs than the big-deck outfits. FitRon 45 splashed 23.5 raiders on the afternoon of the 6th, including 3.5 by Jim Cain. Three more splashed the next day, raising Cain's tally to eight. The squadron tallied four more on the 12th and 14th, frequently intercepting suiciders over the radar pickets.

The last day of aerial combat was the 16th, when two divisions engaged a hodge-podge Japanese formation northwest of Okinawa. The eight pilots claimed 14 kills, including four by Lt(jg) Norm Mollard. That action brought the cruise total to 81.5.

Wartime COs:	Cdr. Gordon Schecter +	1 Apr 44
	Lt. Levern E. Forkner	18 Mar 45

Disestablished: 10 Sep 45

VF-46 Men-O-War

Established: 15 Apr 44

Deployment: *Independence* (CVL-22) Mar-Jun 45 F6F-5

Combat record: 27.75 victories. Lost 6 pilots on deployment.
Top scores: Lts. A.T. Morrison and F.D. Fogde, 3 each.

VF-46 was typical of many squadrons established in early 1944. With nearly a year for training and workups, Carl Rooney's outfit was better prepared than any of its adversaries.

Like most air groups in Task Force 38, the Tokyo strikes of February 1945 marked the combat debut of CVLG-44. The new *Independence* Hellcats drew their first blood on the 16th, sharing a Betty with a VF-45 pilot. Another victory that day and three the next were the only aerial shooting for the next month.

Following a lone Jill splashed 19 March, VF-46 returned to Japan proper ten days later. The CO got a Frank confirmed and a probable while three more pilots downed four other bandits over Kagoshima.

Three Zekes were claimed on picket duty 12 April, after which the task group returned to Home waters. On the 15th Lt. Cdr. R.A. Weatherup's division surprised Japanese fighters taking off from Kanoya and bagged four. Postwar evaluation proved that one of Doc Weatherup's two victims was the George of Petty Officer Soichi Sugita, a veteran ace sometimes credited with 120 kills.

Four more victories were added during the rest of the month, three on the 17th and one on the 22nd.

FitRon 46's last combat came over Kikai Shima on 4 May. Three pilots claimed six kills, raising the total to 27.5 by 19 pilots.

Wartime COs: Cdr. Carl W. Rooney 15 Apr 44

Disestablished: 14 Sep 45

VF-47 Fighting Cocks

Established: 15 May 44

Deployment: *Bataan* (CVL-29) Mar-Aug 45 F6F-5, -5P

Combat record: 67.5 victories, one ace. Losses unknown.
Top score: Lt. Samuel B. Hibbard, 7.33.

The Fighting Cocks of VF-47 got off to a consistent start aboard *Bataan*, claiming 6.5 confirmed and one damaged during their first four days of air combat in March 1945. Lt. Sam Hibbard's team shared two on the 19th, starting the string that would make him the squadron's only ace. The air group lost CAG Walker Ethridge the next day, but by month's end the squadron total stood at 8.5, including four shared by Hibbard.

FitRon 47's first large combat occurred over Kikai Airfield on 3 April, with 10 Japanese fighters credited to 11 pilots. Four more were added over the next eight days, largely the result of CAP intercepts.

The Fighting Cocks' biggest day of the war was 16 April, when the *kamikazes* came out in force. Flying standing patrols north of Okinawa, eight pilots splashed 23 in a half hour. Five scored multiples, including three each by Lts(jg) Bob Wallace and Harry Losson. Sam Hibbard ran his score to 5.33.

Over the next week three more victories were logged, bringing the April total to 40.

The next big combat occurred when 14 pilots claimed an equal number of kills north of Okinawa on 11 May. Ens. Bill Elder led the scoring with 2.5 Tojos.

Fighting 47 downed two Zekes on 14 May and split another, then claimed another pair ten days later, including one by Hibbard. The last victory came 60 days thereafter, when Lt(jg) Bob Wallace split a Zeke with an unknown squadron.

In all, 33 pilots contributed to the total 67.5 victories, with 16 of those amounting to 49.5. Behind Hibbard were Ens. Oliver Swisher with 4.83 and Lt(jg) Harry Losson with 4.

Wartime CO: Cdr. Walker Ethridge + 15 May 44
Lt.Cdr. Albert H. Clancy, Jr. 20 Mar 45

Disestablished: 21 Sep 45

VF-49 Forty-Niners

Established: 10 Aug 44

Deployment: *San Jacinto* (CVL-30) May-Aug 45 F6F-5, -5P

Combat record: 14 victories. No combat losses?
Top score: Lt(jg) Jack A. Anderson, 4.

Established in Seattle a year before cessation of hostilities, VF-49 arrived in WestPac aboard *San Jacinto* in May 1945. The squadron's first two victories were a Myrt and Zeke destroyed over the radar picket line off Okinawa on 25 May, with Ens. Simon Jamouzian claiming the initial kill.

During strikes against Japan on 24 July, six pilots claimed four kills, a probable and a damaged. Most of the bandits were Franks engaged over Bungo Strait.

The seventh victory came on CAP 13 August when Lt(jg) Jack Anderson bagged a Judy—his second kill.

Two days later the Forty-Niners logged their biggest day of the war—and their last. Four pilots downed seven Zekes near Mito Airfield, with Gibson, George Williams and Elwood MacDonald claiming two each. It was the second-greatest tally on "the day the shooting stopped," matched only by VF-31 and exceeded by VF-88.

Wartime CO: Lt.Cdr. George M. Rouzee 17 Aug 44

Disestablished: 27 Nov 45

VF-50 Devil Cats

Established: 10 Aug 43

Deployments: *Bataan* (CVL-29) Apr-Jul 44 F6F-3
Cowpens (CVL-25) Jun-Sep 45 F6F-5, -5P

Combat record: 63 victories, 4 aces. Lost 5 on deployments.
Top score: Lt(jg) Daniel R. Rehm, Jr., 6.

NAS Atlantic City, New Jersey, was a long way from Saipan and Iwo Jima, but VF-50 visited those places and many more during two combat deployments. Taking their name from the F6F (as did VF-9, 19, and 92), the Devil Cats embarked in *Bataan* in the spring of 1944. Twice lucky was Lt. Rolle Lemmon, who shot down a Betty on a morning CAP of 21 April and a Sally that afternoon. There followed six weeks of relative inactivity, until the CO, Lt.Cdr. Johnnie Strange, bagged a Fran on 10 June.

The next day Task Force 58 launched fighter sweeps over the Marianas, and Fighting 50 destroyed four hostiles near Rota: two by Lt. Bruce Barackman and one each by the CO and Ens. Hank Ruda. Barackman and Strange added one more apiece in the next three days.

On CAP the 19th, 11 kills were confirmed, including three by Lt(jg) Dan Rehm while Ens. Bill McCormick, another future ace, also scored. Three more victories came the next day, including two during the dusk attack on the Japanese Mobile Fleet.

Johnnie Strange made ace on the 23rd, then the Devil Cats tackled Iwo Jima on the 24th. Bruce Barackman got two Zekes to become the squadron's second ace while 23 more bandits were claimed destroyed. A return to Iwo on 3 July produced six more kills and two more aces: Dan Rehm and Bill McCormick. The squadron ended the cruise with 61 confirmed kills.

Twelve months passed before Fighting 50 added to its laurels. Flying from *Cowpens*, the squadron recorded two more victories: a Dinah by Lt. Charles Brock on 10 July 1945 and an Oscar by the CO, Raleigh Kirkpatrick, on the 24th.

Wartime COs:	Lt.Cdr. Johnnie C. Strange	10 Aug 43
	Cdr. Raleigh C. Kirkpatrick	1 Oct 44

Disestablished: 29 Oct 45

VF-51

Established: 22 Sep 43

Deployment: *San Jacinto* (CVL-30) Mar-Nov 44 F6F-3, -5

Combat record: 50.5 victories, one ace. Lost 7 on deployment.
Top score: Lt. William R. Maxwell, 7.

Fighting 51 believed in teamwork. Of 51 victories credited, 27 were shared among two or more pilots—undoubtedly the highest ratio of all FitRons. The squadron embarked in March 1944, sailing in *San Jacinto*—"flagship of the Texas Navy."

***San Jacinto*, named for the 1836 battle with Mexico, was called "Flagship of the Texas Navy." Her first fighter squadron was VF-51, engaged in combat from May to October 1944. This F6F-3, over Task Force 58, displays the distinctive X on the rudder which identified "San Jac" aircraft.**

Lt. Bob Maxwell's division scored the first two victories: a Betty and an Emily over the Marianas on 11 June 1944—first day of the campaign leading up to the Turkey Shoot. Maxwell had flown a tour with VF-11 in the Solomons, surviving a midair collision and a long trek to safety with a coastwatcher. Now he hit his stride.

Seven more kills were logged on the 15th, including three by Maxwell, who achieved acedom. On the first day of the carrier battle, 19 June, VF-51 splashed another seven raiders and split an eighth as Cdr. Charlie Moore (previously CO VF-4 in the Atlantic) scored 1.50.

By late July the tally had reached 22.50, but "San Jac" Hellcats lacked further airborne targets until October. In three days from the 10th to 12th, 4.50 more victories were recorded, then came the squadron's best day in combat. On 15 October Moore's pilots splashed nine bandits, followed by two on the 17th and another the 20th.

San Jac search teams hunted Japanese fleet units during the 24th, splashing one Jake floatplane and sharing another with a Torpedo 51 crew. Four Zekes on the 30th closed out the month with 22 victories confirmed.

The deployment drew to a close in November. Three snoopers were destroyed on the 11th, and three more Frans on the 19th, raising the total to 50.5 kills. Of those, only four had been over land, reflecting the CAP role so prominent in CVL FitRon missions.

Wartime COs:	Lt.Cdr. John F. Adams	22 Sep 43
	Lt.Cdr. Thomas B. Bradbury	Nov 43
	Lt.Cdr. Charles L. Moore, Jr.	Feb 44
	Lt.Cdr. William E. Lamb	25 Jan 45

Disestablished: 13 Nov 45

VF-53

Chronology: Established as VF-48 (Jun 44)
Redesignated VF-53 (2 Jan 45)

Deployment: *Saratoga* (CV-3) Jan-Mar 45 F6F-5, -5P

Combat record: 5 victories by 5 pilots. Lost 1 officer.

Air Group 53 was unique in having a both a day- and night-fighter squadron. VF-53 existed as such for less than 90 days and probably had the shortest combat career of any FitRon. First combat came on 16 February 1945 as *Saratoga* supported strikes on the Japanese home islands. Ensigns Mort Murphy and Bob Currier splashed an unidentified fighter near the task force—the air group's only success of the day.

Next stop was Iwo Jima, where Marines went ashore on 19 February. Two days later four pilots splashed four Zekes during a dusk suicide attack, but others got through the CAP. "Sara" was mauled by five hits, forcing her out of action. She never returned to combat.

Wartime CO: Lt.Cdr. R.W. Conrad 2 Jan 45

VF(N)-53 Sleepless Knights

Established: 2 Jan 45

Deployment: *Saratoga* (CV-3) Jan-Mar 45 F6F-5N

Combat record: no victories. No known losses.

One of three squadrons named "The Sleepless Knights," VF(N)-53 was the second FitRon in Air Group 53. The intention was to provide round-the-clock operations, and *Saratoga* was large enough to accommodate the ambitious plan. But Japanese suicide pilots had other ideas, pummeling the big carrier off Iwo Jima on 21 February 1945. Escort carrier *Bismarck Sea* was sunk in the same attack.

In order to employ some suddenly-unused expertise, several of Lt.Cdr. Al Main's pilots transferred to VF(N)-90 in *Enterprise.*

Wartime CO: Lt.Cdr. Alphonse N. Main

Disestablished: 11 Jun 46

VF-60

Established: 15 Jul 43

Deployment: *Santee* (CVE-29) Nov 43-Oct 44 F6F-3

Combat record: 25 victories. Losses unknown.
Top score: Lt(jg) Royce A. Singleton, 3.25

The most successful of 10 Navy F6F squadrons deployed in escort carriers, VF-60 spent almost a year aboard *Santee*. Lt. Ed Dashiell, Jr., scored the first victory when he splashed an Emily seaplane on 19 November 1943. Seven months later, Lt(jg) Royce Singleton bagged a Betty—the first of 3.25 kills which would make him the squadron's top scorer. Five days after, on 22 June 1944, a Judy was destroyed. A drought then lasted until mid-October, when *Santee* participated in the Philippines campaign. Ens. Billie McManemin scored a probable Val on the 18th and shared a Tony the next day.

Three fights over Leyte Gulf occupied Fighting 60 through the 24th, with seven Lily bombers destroyed that morning. Two each were credited to Royce Singleton and Ens. Ralph Kalal. Two Zekes and a Jake floatplane were added later in the day.

On the morning of the 25th, three Zekes went into Ormoc Bay, and that afternoon five assorted types were shot into San Bernardino Strait. Fighting 60 closed its victory log the morning of the 26th when three Oscars were destroyed over the same area, two being credited to Lt(jg) Quinn LaFargue.

Following Royce Singleton, the 20 kills were evenly distributed among the pilots, with four claiming 2.0 to 2.5 victories apiece and 11 more with singles or shares. The squadron reformed at Seattle in January 1945.

Wartime COs: Lt.Cdr. H.O. Feilbach Jul 43

Disestablished: 19 Nov 45

VF(N)-63 Sleepless Knights

Established: 20 Jun 45

Deployment: *Kula Gulf* (CVE-108) Aug-Sep 45 F6F-5N

Combat record: No victories, no known losses.

Night Fighting 63 shared the "Sleepless Knights" name of VF(N)-53, but had even less opportunity for combat than the short-lived *Saratoga* squadron. In fact, documentation for VF(N)-63 is so sketchy that not even the name of the commanding officer survives in Navy archives.

Established six weeks before the end of hostilities, FitRon 63 boarded the escort carrier *Kula Gulf* and briefly flew missions in the Western Pacific. The squadron was disestablshed less than six months after standing up.

Wartime CO: Unknown

Disestablished 11 Dec 45

VF-71

Chronology: Established as VB-7 (7 Jul 39)
Redesignated VF-71 (1 Jul 40)

Deployment: *Wasp* (CV-7) Dec 41-Sep 42 F4F-3, -4

Combat record: 7 victories. Lost 4 officers, 8 enlisted.
Top score: Lt. Carl W. Rooney, 2.50 (3.50).

Fighting 71 was ashore on 7 December, awaiting F4F-4s. Heavily reinforced with transfers from three other fighting squadrons, the unit built up to 29 aircraft and 37 pilots well before any other VF squadron.

In March 1942, when *Wasp* sailed to Britain for brief service in the Mediterranean, most of the air group went ashore at RNAS Hatston. Though 47 RAF Spitfires were loaded aboard for delivery to Malta, 19 Wildcats were kept by VF-72. The British fighters were flown off 20 April, and upon return to the U.K., VF-71 relieved Fighting 72 for the next Malta trip.

Back in Norfolk by June, *Wasp* proceeded to San Diego via the Panama Canal, then on to Hawaii and points west. The air group's first genuine combat came on 7 August, covering the Guadalcanal landings. Court Shands' pilots strafed Japanese floatplanes at Tulagi, but *Wasp's* two SBD squadrons claimed seven aerial victories before either Wildcat outfit had a chance. VF-71's initial shootdown was a patrol plane splashed 27 August, followed by a second on 15 September, but the ship was torpedoed and sunk that day.

Temporarily based at Espiritu Santo, New Hebrides, VF-71 began reinforcing the hard-pressed VF-5 on Guadalcanal. Lt. Pat Rooney's detachment flew with Lt.Cdr. Roy Simpler's squadron, gaining five more confirmed and two probable victories in October. When VF-5 departed "Cactus," the Fighting 71 contingent joined the Marines of VMF-121. *Wasp's* displaced orphans finally left Guadalcanal by 3 November.

Wartime CO: Lt.Cdr. Courtney Shands 21 Mar 42

Disestablished: 7 Jan 43

VF-72 Fighting Wasps

Chronology: Established as VF-7 (1 Jul 39)
Redesignated VF-72 (1 Jul 40)

Deployments:	*Ranger* (CV-4)	Dec 41-Mar 42	F4F-3
	Saratoga (CV-3)	Jun-Jul 42	F4F-4
	Hornet (CV-8)	Jul-Oct 42	F4F-4
	Guadalcanal	Feb-Mar 43	F4F-4

Combat record: 44 victories, one ace. Lost 6 pilots.
Top score: Ens. George W. Wrenn, 5.25

Originally a *Wasp* squadron, VF-72 was aboard *Ranger* from late December 1941 to mid-March 1942. Like sister squadron VF-71, Courtney Shands' unit rode *Wasp* to the Mediterranean, reinforcing Britain's Malta garrison. However, Shands was relieved by Lt.Cdr. Mike Sanchez in March, and remained at the helm for the rest of the squadron's history. Shands then took over VF-71.

Upon *Wasp's* arrival in Hawaii, a VF-72 detachment participated in *Saratoga's* Midway reinforcement. No combat occurred, however, until the Tulagi-Guadalcanal landings 20 August. When *Wasp* was sunk in September, VF-72 was assigned to relieve *Hornet's* shattered VF-8. Flying missions near the Solomons, Fighting 72 broke into the score column with four snoopers splashed on 5 October.

Hank Sanchez's pilots found additional combat in the first half of October, claiming four more Japanese aircraft in support of operations near Guadalcnal. But the main test came at Santa Cruz where, between strike escort and CAPs, VF-72 claimed 30 confirmed and 15 probable victories. Despite the Wildcats' best efforts, *Hornet* was sunk by Japanese carrier planes, but not before producing her only ace: Ens. George W. Wrenn. The tall southerner claimed five attackers in one mission of 26 October.

Eight VF-72 veterans joined *Enterprise's* Fighting 10 in November while others spread their experience throughout three CVE squadrons in the Solomons.

Subsequently land-based, VF-72 scored six more kills during a mission off New Georgia on 4 February 1943.

Wartime COs:	Lt.Cdr. Courtney Shands	Jul 41
	Lt.Cdr. Henry G. Sanchez	21 Mar 42

Disestablished: 29 Mar 43

VF-74 (I) Flying Wolfhounds

Established: 25 Mar 44

Deployment: *Kasaan Bay* (CVE-69) Jun-Sep 44 F6F-5

Combat record: 2 victories. Lost 5 pilots on deployment.
Top score: Lt(jg) E.W. Castanedo, 0.75.

One of three U.S. Navy fighter squadrons to fly combat in Europe, the Wolfhounds were formed at NAS Norfolk in March 1944. They boarded *Kasaan Bay* in June, bound for the Mediterranean to support the Anglo-American invasion of southern France. Teamed with VOF-1 in *Tulagi*, Fighting 74 also had a small night-fighter detachment on Corsica.

"D-Day South" was 15 August, but aerial opposition was nonexistant. No Luftwaffe fighters were encountered, though VF-74 shot down a Ju-88 and Do-217 on the 19th. The CO was killed the next day, however, as was another pilot. German flak, always formidable, took a toll of carrier planes as well as Allied air force aircraft. Upon return to the U.S., VF-74 was disestablished 1 October.

Another VF-74 was established in 1945, intended for one of the new Midway-class carriers.

A short-lived squadron, VF-74 only existed from March to October 1944. This F6F-5, carrying a bomb load, prepares to launch from *Kasaan Bay* in support of Operation Anvil-Dragoon during August—the unit's only combat. During the invasion of Southern France VF-74 lost five pilots, including the CO, Lt.Cdr. H.B. Bass, in 432 sorties.

Wartime COs:	Lt. R.C. Stapler	25 Mar 44
	Lt.Cdr. Harry B. Bass +	11 Apr 44
	Lt. H.H. Bassore	20 Aug 44
	Lt.Cdr. J.H. Sandor	Sep 44

Disestablished: 1 Oct 44

VF(N)-75

Established: 1 Apr 43

Deployment: Solomons Oct 43-early 44 F4U-2, F6F-3

Combat record: 7 victories. No losses.
Top score: Lts H.D. O'Neil, Jr., J.S. Hill, and R.L. Johns, 2 each.

Led by the flamboyant Lt.Cdr. Gus Widhelm, VF(N)-75 was one of only two Navy night-fighter squadrons equipped with Corsairs in WW II. Though designated F4U-2, the night-fighting Corsair probably should have been the F4U-1N, owing to its AIA radar. In any event, this little-known unit inaugurated the F4U to Navy combat, beating VF-17 to the scoring column by eight hours.

The first success came on the night of 31 October when Lt. Danny O'Neill shot down a Betty near the Shortland Islands. He repeated with another Betty on 11 December. Three more confirmed and a probable came that month, all by Lt. John Hill. Lt. Charlie Penner claimed a confirmed and a probable, then Lt. Reuben Johns made it a three-way tie for top score when he gained his second victory—the squadron's last—on 13 January 1944.

A segment of VF(N)-75 went to the Fast Carrier Task Force that same month, designated VF(N)-101 under Lt.Cdr. Chick Harmer.

Wartime CO:	Lt.Cdr. William J. Widhelm	1 Apr 43
	Lt. Hugh D. O'Neill, Jr.	Mar 44

Disestablished: 2 Oct 44

VF(N)-76

Established: 15 Jul 43

Deployments: *Essex* (CV-9), *Yorktown* (CV-10), *Hornet* (CV-12), *Lexington* (CV-16), and *Bunker Hill* (CV-17), detachments, early to mid 1944. F6F-3E/N, -5N

Combat record: 37 victories, 3 aces. Lost 3 officers.
Top score: Lt. Russell L. Reiserer, 8 (9).

A plane director guides a VF(N)-76 "Det 3" Hellcat up *Essex*'s flight deck on 10 May 1944. Flying mainly F6F-3Ns, Lt.Cdr. Pete Aurand's squadron also provided night fighter detachments to four other carriers, claiming 37 kills between February and September. Day FitRons absorbed most VF(N) teams in October, providing an organic night capability in all CV-9 class ships.

As the first Hellcat night fighting squadron, VF(N)-76 conducted five months of accelerated training on the East Coast. Then, under former SBD pilot Pete Aurand, Fighting 76 raced across the U.S. and most of the Pacific to reach the Fast Carrier Task Force in time for the Marshalls operation, all in less than a month.

Aurand led the squadron's first launch from *Bunker Hill* on 29 January—just 26 days out of Quonset Point. His team first bled the enemy during the morning of 22 February, downing six bandits in barely an hour. The CO got the first kill, with Ens. Jack Bertie claiming three.

Aurand scored again in April, and the squadron's eighth kill was logged in the Marianas on 15 June.

Former VF-10 pilot Russ Reiserer's Det Two was by far the most successful of all VF(N) detachments, claiming 25 victories aboard *Yorktown* and *Hornet* from April to September 1944. Dear and Dungan, with seven each, were close behind the skipper, who had previous combat with VF-10. For a night owl, Reiserer had a very good day on 19 June when he shot down five Vals over Guam. Other pilots splashed four more.

Lt(jg)s Fred Dungan and John Dear stirred up a nocturnal hornet's nest at Chichi Jima in the Bonins in the predawn of 4 July. Despite damage to both Hellcats and Dungan's wounds, the pair shot down seven enemy float fighters. Two more night kills came on the 7th; one by Reiserer.

Two additional successes in September concluded the squadron's scoring. The last fell to John Dear on the 22nd in Philippine waters. About 10 of the squadron's 37 kills were made in darkness.

Pete Aurand retired as a vice admiral, widely known for innovative approaches to night fighting and antisubmarine warfare.

Wartime CO: Lt.Cdr. Evan P. Aurand 15 Jul 43

Disestablished: 6 Nov 44

VF(N)-77

Established: 1 Dec 43

Deployments: *Essex* (CV-9), *Yorktown* (CV-10), *Franklin* (CV-13), and *Wasp* (CV-14) detachments, early to mid-1944. F6F-3E/N

Combat record: 8 victories. Lost 1 pilot on deployment.
Top scores: Lt. A.C. Benjes, Jr., and Ens. G.T. Tarleton, 2 each.

The urgency of Project Afirm, the Navy night-fighter program, may be judged by the fact that Fighting 77 scored its first victories barely six months after establishing. The pattern was similar in other VF(N) units, as nocturnal defense of carrier task forces received high priority.

Lt.Cdr. Bob Freeman's detachments were unique in that all their kills were made in the dark. First blood went to the CO's *Essex* det over Agana, Guam, on 20 June 1944. In the predawn hours, Freeman claimed two Vals and Ens. George Tarleton another—all in 20 minutes.

Four more successes were logged during four nights spanning two weeks in July. Ens. Joe Rohde and Lt. Tony Benjes off *Yorktown* splashed a Rufe and Betty on the 4th and 11th, respectively. Then, on the 12th and 16th, Ens. Charlie Soderlund and Lt. John Boyum put *Wasp* on the board with an Emily and an unidentified bogey. The latter three kills were the only ones credited in Task Force 58 between 9 and 24 July.

Finally, Tony Benjes, having moved to *Franklin*, downed an Emily on 1 September.

Wartime CO: Lt.Cdr. Robert M. Freeman 1 Dec 43

Disestablished: 25 Sep 44

VF(N)-78

Established: 1 Feb 44

Deployments: *Enterprise* (CV-6) and *Intrepid* (CV-11), early 1944. F6F-3E/N

Combat record: 2 victories. No losses.
Top score: Lt. W.H.B. Miller, 1.

Formed at Quonset Point, R.I., in early 1944, VF(N)-78's reached combat that summer with detachments in *Enterprise* and *Intrepid*. Thus, they succeeded Chick Harmer's Corsairs after VF(N)-101 rotated home.

The skipper was Cdr. Jim Gray, who had led Fighting Six from The Big E at Midway. He logged VF(N)-78's initial intercept when he damaged a Betty near Iwo Jima early in the morning of 31 August.

Only two more combats occurred before the squadron was absorbed by Air Group 20. Approaching the Philippines on 12 September, Lts. Bill Millar and Don Matheson splashed a Frances in daylight. Ten days later three pilots combined to destroy one Zeke and damage another, brining the squadron record to two confirmed and two damaged.

In accordance with revised air group organization, on 2 October the *Enterprise* det became VF-20's organic night fighter team. Jim Gray later commanded the squadron after Cdr. Fred Bakutis was shot down and temporarily missing in the Sulu Sea late that month.

Wartime CO: Cdr. James S. Gray 1 Feb 44

Disestablished: 2 Oct 44

VF-80 Vorse's Vipers

Established: 1 Feb 44

Deployment:			
	Ticonderoga (CV-14)	Nov 44-Jan 45	F6F-5, -5N, -5P
	Hancock (CV-19)	Jan-Mar 45	F6F-5, -5N, -5P

Combat record: 159.5 victories, 10 aces. Lost 14 officers.
Top score: Lt. Patrick D. Fleming, 10 (19).

Established in Atlantic City, *Ticonderoga's* original FitRon was known as "Vorse's Vipers" after the first skipper, Lt.Cdr. Albert "Scoop" Vorse. Already an ace from 1942 action in F4Fs, Vorse welded the squadron into a combat-ready team by the time "Tico" arrived in Philippine waters in November 1944. However, by then he had fleeted up to CAG, resulting in Lt.Cdr. "Pete" Keith, exec of VF-81, taking over on 16 October.

A pair of aces, Pat Fleming (left) and Zeke Cormier in the VF-80 ready room on *Ticonderoga* late in 1944.

Throttle up, head back, a VF-80 pilot awaits a launch by the catapult officer on board *Hancock,* 14 Feb 1945.

The first combat occurred during sweeps of enemy airfields near Manila on 5 November, netting six kills. A dozen more on the 25th raised the Vipers' score to 22.5. The only combat of December again occurred over the Philippines on the 14th, resulting in 21 kills. Lt. Bob Anderson claimed five fighters while Lt. Pat Fleming and his section leader, Zeke Cormier, each bagged four.

VBF-80 was established on 10 January, but air group records make little distinction between the fighter squadrons. Formosa ops in January brought 29 additional kills, but Tico sustained heavy *kamikaze* damage on the 21st. Upon return to the fleet anchorage at Ulithi, CVG-80 transferred to *Hancock* in time for the historic strikes against Japan proper.

"Hanna's" new fighters made a sensational debut in CV-19 when, on 16 February, four combats resulted in 72 confirmed and 16 probables. Pete Keith, Pat Fleming, Alex Anderson and Bill Edwards all made ace in a day while CAG Vorse nailed four. It established a new record in Naval Aviation.

A dozen more kills came the next day, with Fleming downing four Nates. The last three kills occurred on 1 March, by which time 56 pilots had scored 159.5 victories.

The squadron reformed in May with Fleming as skipper, but the war ended just four months later.

Wartime COs:	Lt.Cdr. Albert O. Vorse	1 Feb 44
	Lt.Cdr. Leroy W. Keith	16 Oct 44
	Lt.Cdr. Patrick D. Fleming	May 45

Disestablished: 16 Sep 46

VBF-80

Established: 10 Jan 45

Deployment: *Ticonderoga* (CV-14) Jan 45 F6F-5
Hancock (CV-19) Jan-Mar 45 F6F-5

Combat record: unknown share of VF-80's 159. Losses unknown.
Top score: Lt. Patrick D. Fleming, 9 (19)

Established at sea aboard *Ticonderoga*, VBF-80 was led by Lt.Cdr. Frank Gooding with Lt. Pat Fleming as executive officer.

Air Group 80 seems to have been unusual in that little distinction existed between the fighters and fighter-bombers, other than administrative workloads. Consequently, the original Vipers retained their identity even when half the squadron officially functioned as another organization.

Off Formosa on 21 January 1945, "Tico" was struck by two *kamikazes*. The damage was not immediately repairable, requiring the air group to transfer to *Hancock* in Ulithi anchorage before month's end. Subsequent operations included the Tokyo strikes, Iwo Jima, return visits to the Philippines, and more Home Island operations.

At the end of the *Hancock* cruise, Zeke Cormier and a few others wanted to transfer to VF-82 in *Bennington*. However, the requests were denied and the air group returned to the West Coast intact.

Wartime CO: Lt.Cdr. Frank Gooding 10 Jan 45

Disestablished: 16 Sep 45

VF-81 Freelancers

Established: 2 Mar 44

Deployment: *Wasp* (CV-14) Nov 44-Mar 45 F6F-5, -5N, -5P

Combat record: 43 victories, one ace. Lost 18 on deployment.
Top score: Lt(jg) Hugh V. Sherrill, 5.50

Fighting 81 completed its first year of existence by finishing its combat tour 12 months after establishing. Initial combat from *Wasp* came on 14 November 1944 when Lt(jg) Harold Metzger shot a Zeke into Manila Bay. Thirty days later CAG Fred Brush and two other pilots added three more successes over the Philippines. Among the victors was Lt(jg) Hugh Sherrill, destined to become the squadron's only ace.

Based aboard *Wasp* (CV-18), this VF-81 Hellcat made an unscheduled stop aboard *Belleau Wood* in early 1945. On 1 January the Freelancers were the largest carrier squadron afloat, with 90 F6Fs owing to displacement of Bombing 81 and reducing the torpedo squadron to 15 TBMs. However, with arrival of two Marine Corsair squadrons the Freelancers reverted to 36 Hellcats for the remainder of their deployment.

Another pair of Zekes succumbed to VF-81 during Formosa strikes on 4 January 1945, with six more victories over Formosa and the China coast by month's end.

Operations over Japan occupied the rest of FitRon 81's combat. The biggest day of the deployment occurred over Tokyo on 16 February, when *Wasp* Hellcats claimed 15 confirmed and four probables. The next day 11 more confirmed and three probables were added, including two Zekes, a Tony and a Tojo by Sherrill.

Return strikes on the 25th brought the squadron's last four victories: a total of 43 compiled by 31 pilots.

Wartime CO:	Lt.Cdr. F.K. Upham	2 Mar 44
	Lt.Cdr. Harvey P. Lanham	6 Feb 45

Subsequent record: Redesignated VF-13A (1946), VF-131 (1948), VF-64 (1949), VF-21 (1959). Still flying F-14s in 1995.

VF-82

Established: 1 Apr 44

Deployment: *Bennington* (CV-20) Sep 44-Jun 45 F6F-5, -5N, -5P

Combat record: 85 victories, 5 aces. Lost 15 pilots on deployment.
Top score: Lt. Robert H. Jennings, 7 (9.5)

Fighting 82 deployed in *Bennington* with more experienced pilots than most squadrons in 1944. The skipper, Lt.Cdr. Ed Hessel, had two confirmed victories from VF-72, as did Lt. Bob Jennings. Armand Manson similarly had two kills from VF-18's 1943 cruise.

Five months after reporting aboard, VF-82 finally got a shot at airborne hostiles. Lt. Buck Gregory's division tangled with Japanese fighters near Atsugi, claiming six destroyed. Four more were bagged overland the next day.

The next dogfight was a month later when four additional victories were claimed at Kanoya East on 18 March. Returning to the hunting grounds of Kanoya and Kure the following day, VF-81 notched five more kills. That tally was matched the 28th when Armand Manson and Ens. Jack Turner caught a Nell bomber towing a glider—perhaps the only such kill in the Pacific.

By 2 April the *Bennington* Hellcats had logged 27 victories since mid-February. They doubled their score with 27 kills on 6 April, the day the *kamikazes* swarmed over Ie Shima near Okinawa. Gregory, Jennings, and Clarence Davies all made their fifth kills of the cruise that day. Six more victories came on the 7th, then nine on the 12th, when Manson made ace, but top score was Lt(jg) Ray Klingerman splashed four bombers—his only score of the war.

Eight more victories came in three days, 14-16 April, ending the month with fifty-three confirmed and three damaged.

Ens. John Hoag became the squadron's fifth ace when he killed three fighters over Izumi Airfield, Japan, on 13 May. VF-81 closed its victory log with three more kills near Kagoshima Bay on the 14th. A sixth ace to fly with the squadron was Lt. Ken Smith, a night fighter who logged two victories while temporarily detached from *Enterprise's* VF(N)-90.

Wartime CO: Lt.Cdr. Edward W. Hessell 1 Apr 44

Subsequent record: Redesignated VF-17A (1946), VF-171 (1948).

Disestablished 1958

In Feb '45, Ens. J.U. Matura, of VF-82 missed all the wires on *Bennington* , but despite this disastrous dive into the ocean he got free and was rescued by destroyer *John Rodgers.*

VF-83 Kangaroos

Established: 1 May 1944

Deployment: *Essex* (CV-9) Mar-Sep 45 F6F-5, -5N, -5P

Combat record: 137 victories, 11 aces. Lost 6 pilots on deployment.
Top score Lt. Thaddeus T. Coleman 8 (10)

"Pug" Southerland was an Annapolis graduate who had survived a combat with top Japanese ace Saburo Sakai while flying with VF-5 over Guadalcanal. He would prove an apt teacher, as nearly a dozen of his Fighting 83 pilots would themselves become aces.

Shortly after arriving in WestPac in March 1945, Southerland was transferred to *Langley* as CAG-23, being replaced by H.A. Sampson. Meanwhile, the Kangaroos claimed their first nine victories over Japanese airfields on the 19th. Three more kills were scored in the rest of the month.

Persistent suicide attacks in April resulted in numerous intercepts off Okinawa. Sixteen raiders were splashed on the 3rd, with Thad Coleman becoming VF-83's first ace. However, the 6th brought unprecedented exposure to *kamikazes*. In five actions, 56 raiders were claimed destroyed while four pilots made ace: Jim Barnes, Hugh Batten, Sam Brocato, and Larry Clark. The major fight was a 90-minute brawl over Amami and Tokuno Shimas, with 26 kills were logged. At day's end, VF-83 had made the third-highest killing of a single Navy squadron in the war.

Four more victories came in the next two days, then Bob Hamilton and Bill Kingston made ace over Ie Shima on 12 April. Nine more kills were achieved by month's end, when VF-83's tally had risen to 106. All but 11 of those fell in April.

F6F Hellcats of VF-83, armed with rockets, prepare to launch from *Essex* for a strike in 1945.

Twenty-four suiciders were splashed on 4 May as two divisions tied into a mixture of obsolete and modern combat types as well as trainers. Eight pilots scored, with three becoming aces over Izema Shima: Don McPherson, Lyttleton Ward, and Myron Truax, who got six to become the squadron's last ace.

Don Umphres, a night fighter, got two in the predawn hours of 13 May while Jim Barnes got another.

The last three kills came early on the morning of 28 July when Batten, Brocato, and Ens. Clyde Clark each bagged a Tony over Metatsubara Airfield.

Wartime COs: Cdr. James J. Southerland 1 May 44
Lt.Cdr. H.A. Sampson Apr 45

Disestablished: 24 Sep 45

VBF-83

Established: 6 Jan 45

Deployment: *Essex* (CV-9) Mar-Sep 45 F4U-1D, FG-1D

Combat record: 91 victories, 3 aces. Losses unknown.
Top score: Lt. Thomas H. Reidy, 10

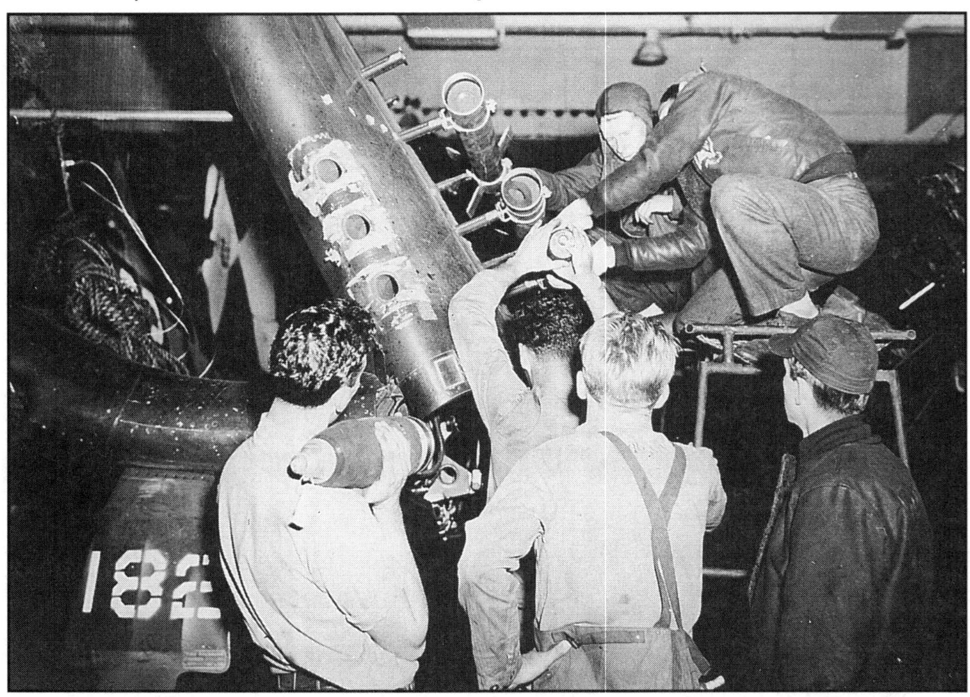

VBF-83 aboard *Essex* was equipped with Vought F4U Corsairs, seen here being loaded with 5 inch rockets on the hangar deck, 27 Mar 45.

Fighting-Bombing 83 beat its VF counterpart to the scoring column by downing 18 Japanese planes on 18 March 1945. Fifteen pilots claimed kills, including two each by future aces Tom Reidy and Lindley Godson. By month's end the tally stood at 25.

On 6 April—the day the VF squadron splashed 56—the Corsairs claimed a baker's dozen, mainly over Amami and Tokuno Shimas north of Okinawa. Seven kills were scored both on the 7th and 12th, with Reidy becoming the first ace in a fight with Oscars on the 15th. In all, the squadron claimed 40 victories during April.

The next big fight was near Okinawa on 5 May, with Bob Kincaid making ace with thee of 14 victories that day. Eight more kills went into the squadron log by the 20th.

Unique among all Navy aces was the squadron's Lt. W.H. Harris, who scored his first victory as a VB-17 SB2C pilot. He added four more while flying Corsairs, the last on 28 July. Tragically, he was lost on 9 August when his bomb exploded in flight. The cease-fire went into effect six days later. Tom Reidy brought the squadron tally to 91 with his tenth personal victory on 15 August, the first of 34 shootdowns on the day the shooting stopped.

Wartime CO: Lt.Cdr. Frank A. Patriarca 6 Jan 45

Disestablished: 24 Sep 45

A VBF-83 F4U-1D folds its wings en route to *Essex*'s parking area following recovery on 19 April 1945. The squadron's 91st and last victory was also the 10th of Lt. T. Hamil Reidy, who splashed a Myrt reconnaissance bomber near the task force on 15 August 1945—the day hostilities ceased.

A Corsair of VF-84 launches from CV-17, *Bunker Hill* 8 Feb 45 for a raid on Tokyo.

VF-84 Wolf Gang

Established: 1 May 44

Deployment: *Bunker Hill* (CV-17) Jan-Jun 45 F4U-1D, F6F-5N, -5P

Combat record: 137 victories, 4 aces. Lost 25 officers, 3 EM.
Top scores: Lt. Doris C. Freeman and John Gildea, 7 each.

When VF-84 stood up at NAS North Island, it was heavy with VF-17 talent. From skipper Rog Hedrick on down, the likes of Chico Freeman and John Smith were less than 60 days removed from combat in the Solomons.

Upon arrival in WestPac, CVG-84 was one of a few air groups with all-Corsair fighters, as VMF-221 and 451 also deployed. First combat was the two-day Tokyo strike in February 1945, with Lt(jg) Jim Dixon opening the Wolf Gang's victory log when he splashed a Helen the morning of the 16th. Five more kills that day and five the next provided a solid start to the cruise. Upon return to Empire waters eight days later, Fighting 84 added nine more victories. Hedrick bagged three, for a wartime total of 12.

CAG-84, Cdr. G.M. Ottinger, was killed by flak off Okinawa on 24 March. Rog Hedrick thereafter assumed duties as air group commander, but the paperwork was not complete until 27 April. His exec, Lt.Cdr. Raymond "Ted" Hill, moved up to CO FitRon 84.

April was the busiest month of the cruise, with aerial combat on 13 days. Heaviest activity occurred on the 12th, with eight kills, and the 28th, with a record 20 shootdowns over Kikai Shima. In all, Okinawa operations resulted in 58 victories during April.

The squadron's first three aces were crowned that month: John Gildea on the 6th; Willis Laney the 11th and Chico Freeman the 28th (not counting two prior with VF-17).

Combat continued into May, with four kills on the 4th. Action peaked a week later with 11 more victories as John Smith scored his fifth kill of the cruise on the 11th (he had three prior with VF-17), as did Lt(jg) Lew Maberry. Four Marine pilots also made ace.

However, that morning *Bunker Hill* was savaged by two *kamikazes*, resulting in survivable damage exceeded only by *Franklin's*. Among 389 killed were 22 from VF-84. The cruise total of 137 KIAs among all five squadrons was second only to Air Group Five's combined losses aboard *Yorktown* (CV-10) and *Franklin*.

Lost among the Corsair's success in CVG-84 was the night fighter detachment, with six Hellcat pilots accounting for as many as 11 kills.

Ted Hill reformed the squadron in July, re-equipped with F6Fs, but the war ended before VF-84 could depart Los Alamitos.

Wartime COs:	Lt.Cdr. Roger R. Hedrick	5 May 44
	Lt.Cdr. Raymond E. Hill	27 Apr 45

Disestablished: 8 Oct 45

VF-85 Sky Pirates

Established: 15 May 44

Deployment: *Shangri-La* (CV-38) Jan-Sep 45 F4U-1D, F6F-5N, -5P

Combat record: 40 victories. Lost 8 pilots on deployment.
Top score: Lt(jg) Robert A. Bloomfield, 4.

Fighting 85's skipper Warren Ford was an old hand around the Pacific, with victories in VF-8 and VF-72 aboard the original *Hornet*. When the Sky Pirates took their Corsairs aboard the new *Shangri-La* in January 1945, the complexion of the war was vastly changed from when Ford had flown at Midway and Santa Cruz.

The squadron's first kill was a Betty by Ens. John Patton on 29 April. Five days later, near Iheya Shima, seven pilots tied into a flock of floatplanes and Zekes, claiming 13 destroyed. Lt(jg) Paul Chernoff gunned three Zekes while Ens. Walt Green bagged two Petes. It was the squadron's biggest day of the war.

The next big fight occurred 11 May, when the Pirates intercepted several Zekes Southeast of Tori Shima. The F4Us splashed eight plus one Jill, with Lt. Joe Robbins claiming two.

Okinawa and environs remained the center of attraction, as VF-85 again climed nine victories on 28 May. During a four-hour CAP early that morning, an eclectic mixture of Zekes, Oscars, Nicks and Franks was encountered as Lt(jg) Ken Moos bagged three while Lt. Bob Bloomfield and Lt(jg) Dave Lawhon each got a pair.

Over Kagoshima Bay on 2 June Lt(jg) Bill Clarke destroyed two Japanese fighters. A division claimed a Betty destroyed and damaged on 14 July, with Bloomfield downing an Oscar during strikes on Kobe the 24th. He added a Sally the next day, while other pilots dropped a Topsy transport and a Frank.

With 40 victories, VF-85 was the highest-scoring Navy fighter squadron without an ace. However, Lt. Joe Robbins' total of five included three with VF-85 and Lt(jg) Bob Bloomfield downed four.

Wartime CO: Cdr. Warren W. Ford 15 May 44

Disestablished: 27 Sep 45

VBF-85

Established: 2 Jan 45

Deployment: *Shangri-La* (CV-38) Jan-Aug 45 F4U-1D, FG-1D

Combat record: 10 victories. Lost 9 pilots on deployment.
Top score: Ens. Wallace C. Moessmer, 1.50

Cdr. Birney Strong was among the finest naval aviators of his time, and imparted his passion for perfection to VF-85. He flew SBDs from *Enterprise* for two years, performing exceptionally well at Santa Cruz. Though considered overbearing and egotistical by some, he was also regarded as an excellent instructor. In 1943 he had told one of his VS-10 pilots, "I'm going to make you the second-best dive bomber in the Pacific!"

The squadron's first kill was a Jill split by Lt. Joe Horne and Lt(jg) Glen Chappell near Okinawa on 30 April 1945. Only six other scoring opportunities arose, including Lt. Hugh Horne's division which bagged a Sonia on 28 May. The squadron's best showing came on 3 June when, near Kagoshima, ten claims were made including four fighters destroyed, one probable and five damaged.

Radar picket CAPs on 13 August netted three intercepts, with destruction of a Nick, Grace, and Jill. Again flying RadCAP two days later, Ens. Falvey Sandige splashed a Judy for the last Corsair victory of the war.

VBF-85 was one of the "sharingest" squadrons of the war, as 10 victories were split among 14 pilots, only three of whom had solo kills.

Wartime CO: Cdr. Stockton B. Strong 2 Jan 45

Disestablished: 27 Sep 45

VF-86 Wild Hares

Established: 15 Jun 44

Deployment: *Wasp* (CV-14) Mar, Jun-Sep 45 F6F-5, -5N, -5P

Combat record: 12 victories. Lost 3 pilots on deployment.
Top score: Lt. Armind T. Holderman, 2.

Formed at NAS Atlantic City, FitRon 86 dubbed itself the Sundowners and gained approval of the name in November 1944. Then, someone in BuAer finally realized that VF-11 had taken that name during two combat tours. Consequently, VF-86 became the Wild Hares in June 1945, aboard *Wasp* in WestPac.

The skipper was Cleo Dobson, who had flown an *Enterprise* SBD into the Pearl Harbor attack in 1941. Transferring to fighters, he formed VF-86 at Atlantic City in June 1944 and took the Hares to WestPac aboard *Wasp*, beginning operations 13 March 1945. Five days later Lt(jg) Jim Lansing splashed a Judy for the squadron's first victory. Next morning, the 19th, Ens. Bob Wolford dropped another Judy but more raiders got through the CAP, and *Wasp* sustained serious bomb damage. While withdrawing from enemy waters on the 21st, three pilots each splashed a Fran 30 miles north of the stricken carrier.

Wasp returned to combat in mid-June, but hunting had thinned out. The next victory occurred over Japan on 28 July as Lt. Armind Holderman downed a Frank. He added a Grace overhead the ship on 9 August as well.

On 13 August three more kills were scored during strikes around Inubo Saki Point, Honshu.

Two days later Japan agreed to surrender, but the shooting wasn't over. Early the afternoon of the 15th Lt(jg) Ed Myers bagged a Zeke. A half-hour later, Cleo Dobson, erstwhile dive bomber pilot, finally got his shot at an airborne bandit. Flying CAP with Lt(jg) Jack Morrison, he chased down a Judy and destroyed it—the next-to-last shootdown of the Second World War.

Wartime COs:	Lt.Cdr. Horace E. Tennes	Jun 44
	Lt.Cdr. Cleo J. Dobson	12 Jan 45

Disestablished: 21 Nov 45

VBF-86 Vapor Trails

Established: 3 Jan 45

Deployment: *Wasp* (CV-14) Mar, Jun-Sep 45 F4U-4

Combat record: 7 victories. Lost one pilot on deployment.
Top score: Ens. Richard F. Wear, 2.

Lt.Cdr. Horace Tennes was an expert aviator who had learned to fly before joining the Navy. Previously skipper of VF-86, his *Wasp* BombFitRon was further distinguished as one of only five squadrons to fly carrier-based F4U-4s in combat during WW II.

VBF-86 got off to a good start aboard *Wasp*. Ens. Dick Wear downed a Nakajima Myrt 40 miles southwest of the task group on 18 March 1945, then added a Mitsubishi Betty the next day. Three other pilots also scored on the 19th, the day *Wasp* sustained serious bomb damage with more than 370 casualties.

Sensing a kill, the Japanese pressed their advantage, seeking to finish off *Wasp* before she steamed out of range. But Ens. Mitchell Flint splashed a Myrt snooper on the 20th, the Pippers' sixth kill.

Upon returning to combat in June, VBF-86 had only one more chance at airborne hostiles. During the noon hour of 8 August, Lt. Liburn Edmonston caught a Nick twin-engine recon plane 75 miles from the task force and shot it down. He became the sixth pilot contributing to the squadron's record of seven aerial victories.

Wartime CO: Lt.Cdr. Horace E. Tennes 12 Jan 45

Disestablished: 21 Nov 45

VF-87

Established: 1 Jul 44

Deployment: *Ticonderoga* (CV-14) May-Sep 45 F6F-5, -5N, -5P

Combat record: no victories. Lost 2 pilots on deployment.

Reporting aboard *Ticonderoga* in May 1945, CVG-87 was that carrier's first air group since CVG-80 was forced ashore owing to *kamikaze* damage in January. However, aerial opposition was negligible through the summer of 1945.

Of the combat FitRons without victory claims in WW II, two were night fighters and two were land-based in bypassed areas of the Solomons and Marshalls. VF-87 flew combat from mid May until after VJ-Day, a three-month period when all Navy carrier squadrons claimed just 167 aerial victories. Six of those went to Fighting 87's sister squadron, VBF-87.

Fighting 87 was involved on the last day of hostilities, flying overland strikes against Japan.

Wartime COs: Lt.Cdr. Charles E. Ingalls, Jr. 8 Jul 44

Disestablished: 2 Nov 45

VBF-87

Established: 2 Jan 45

Deployment: *Ticonderoga* (CV-14) May-Sep 45 F6F-5

Combat record: 6 victories. Lost 5 pilots on deployment.
Top score: Lt(jg) K.E. Montague, 1.50

Entering combat late in the war, VBF-87 had only three chances at airborne targets. The first opportunity arose on 6 June 1945 when Lt(jg) Keith Montague's division intercepted three Tonys northwest of Okinawa. Montague splashed one and split another with his wingman, Ens. Glen Doherty. The second section double-teamed the third.

The CO, Porter Maxwell, was killed while attacking Shikoku airfields 24 July. He was succeeded by Lt.Cdr. Walt Haas, who had been one of the star performers in *Yorktown* (CV-5) during 1942. Flying with VF-42 and VF-3, he was credited with 4.83 victories at Coral Sea and Midway.

Four days after Maxwell's death, Lt. Bill Peterson splashed a Jill only seven miles from "Tico." The last two kills were logged by Lt(jg) Bill Hemphill and Ens. Bob Butcher on 13 August.

Two days later VBF-87 may have dropped the last bombs of the war. Lt.Cdr. Charlie Gunnells assigned four of his 12 Hellcats to each of three opportune targets and attacked through low clouds. The last F6Fs were still in their dives when the recall order went out from the task force, and rather than expose themselves to AA gunners, the tail-end Hellcats completed their attacks. Probably the last pilot to bomb Japan was Lt(jg) John McNabb.

Wartime COs:	Cdr. Porter W. Maxwell +	2 Jan 45
	Lt.Cdr. Walter A. Haas	24 Jul 45

Disestablished: 2 Nov 45

VF-88 Gamecocks

Established: 15 Aug 44

Deployment:	Marianas	May-Jun 45	F6F-5
	Yorktown (CV-10)	Jun-Sep 45	F6F-5, -5N, -5P

Combat record: 13 victories. Lost 9 pilots KIA/MIA.
Top score: Lt(jg) Maurice Proctor, 3.

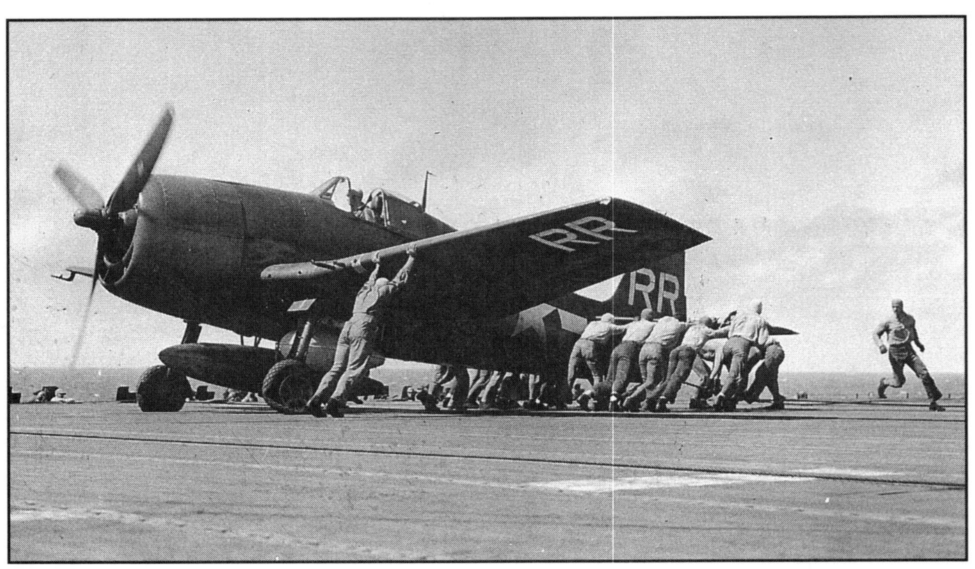

Yorktown **plane handlers position a VF-88 Hellcat for a "deck run" takeoff, 30 July 1945. Two weeks later, in the last major combat of the Second World War, six Gamecocks F6Fs fought an estimated 17 Japanese fighters moments after Tokyo's announcement of surrender on 15 August. The Yorktowners claimed nine kills against four losses.**

Based on Saipan from mid-May to mid-June, FitRon 88 went aboard *Yorktown* on 17 June. Skipper Dick Crommelin was killed in a midair collision over Okinawa on 14 July; his older brother Charlie, CAG-12, had perished in another midair 28 March.

The new CO, Lt. Malcolm "Chris" Cagle, scored the first victory when he downed a Jack over Bungo Strait, Japan, on the 24th. Two Graces were bagged on 9 August by Lt. Bob Appling and Ens. Leonard Komisarek. Four days later Lt(jg) Ray Gonzalez splashed an Irving.

On the morning of 15 August—its first anniversary—Air Group 88 had a strike over Japan when the cease-fire order came through. While outbound over the coast, six VF-88 Hellcats were attacked by a mixed formation of perhaps 17 enemy fighters. Lt(jg) Maury Proctor claimed a Jack and two Franks while Lt(jg) T.W. Hansen bagged a pair of Franks.

Only Proctor and Hansen returned to *Yorktown*. The other four pilots—Lt. Howard Harrison, Lt(jg) Joseph Shaloff, Ens. Wright Hobbs and Eugene Mandeberg—were posthumously credited with one victory each.

In 1982, Proctor and Hansen visited some of the Japanese pilots they fought that day. The Imperial Navy pilots stated that they had not received the cease-fire order, thus resulting in the last dogfight of the Second World War.

Wartime COs:	Lt.Cdr. Richard G. Crommelin +	15 Aug 44
	Lt. Malcolm W. Cagle	14 Jul 45

Disestablished: 29 Oct 45

VBF-88 Gringos

Established: 2 Jan 45

Deployment: *Yorktown* (CV-10) Jun-Sep 45 FG-1D

Combat record: 5 victories, 1 each by five pilots. Lost 9 pilots on deployment.

Established at Otis Field, VBF-88 became the only Corsair squadron to fly from *Yorktown* in WW II. With only three aerial encounters, the Gringos logged five victories over the Japanese home islands during the last three weeks of hostilities.

Lt. Gerald Hennesy bagged an Oscar on the evening of 24 July. Then Lt. Jim Rowney downed a Dinah at sea the afternoon of 8 August.

A long overland strike the morning of the 15th turned up several Myrts at Hokoda Airfield. Lt. Ray McGrath and Lt(jg)s George Lewis and Bob Wohlers each destroyed one of the Nakajima reconnaissance planes.

Before the strike could return to base, Task Force 38 announced that the Japanese had agreed to surrender.

Wartime CO: Lt.Cdr. J.E. Hart 2 Jan 45

Disestablished: 29 Sep 45

An FG-1D Corsair of VBF-88 advances to the launch position on *Yorktown,* 18 Jul 45.

A trio of Grumman F6F-5Ns of VF(N)-90 from *Enterprise* on dusk patrol in 1945.

VF(N)-90 Bats

Chronology: established as VF(N)-103 6 Apr 44
redesignated VF(N)-90 25 Aug 44

Deployment: *Enterprise* (CV-6) Dec 44-May 45 F6F-5N

Combat record: 31 victories. Lost 8 officers on deployment.
Top score: Lt. Owen D. Young, 4.5

When Lt.Cdr. Bob McCullough formed VF(N)-103 at Quonset Point, R.I., he began a process which eventually absorbed three other squadrons. By 25 August 1944, VF(N)-104, -105, and -106 had melded their identity into a new unit which became the VF(N)-90 Bats.

Flying aboard *Enterprise* on Christmas Eve, CAG-90 Bill Martin was back home. As skipper of both Scouting and Torpedo Ten, he was a veteran Big E aviator with extensive night-flying experience.

The Bats' first combat was a triple-header by Lt. Carl Nielsen, who dropped a Dinah, Zeke, and Oscar over the Philippines the afternoon of 6 January 1945. Two more kills were claimed before month's end with another pair during February. Three of these seven successes were scored at night.

Pre-dawn intercepts off Japan on 18 March netted four confirmed and a probable with a kill and a probable the next morning.

Operations around Okinawa brought four successful intercepts during the first half of April, with seven victories credited. One of these on the 11th was the first success for Lt. Ken "KD" Smith, who became a night ace.

By far the biggest single action of the cruise was a series of intercepts over Kagoshima the morning of 12 May. Five Bat pilots downed eight bandits, with Lt. Owen Young accounting for 4.5, his wingman Lt(jg) Charles Latrobe 1.5, and KD Smith and John Kenyon one each.

Next to score was Lt(jg) George Oden, who downed a Dinah before midnight on the 13th. Then Latrobe, Lt(jg)s Lamar Harrison and George Taylor splashed three more bandits during a five-hour stretch in the early morning of the 14th. But at 0730 a lone Zeke dived into the Big E's forward elevator with a 550-pound bomb. After three and a half years, *Enterprise* finally was knocked out of the war.

Not included in VF(N)-90's 31 victories were six more scored by three pilots on detached duty. K.D. Smith became an ace by adding two kills with VF-82's night detachment while Ens. Waldo West bagged three with VF-84 and Lt(jg) Bill Piscopo tagged one while with Smith aboard *Bennington*.

Wartime COs: Lt.Cdr. Robert J. McCullough 5 Apr 44

Disestablished: 21 Jun 46

VF(N)-91

Established: 5 Oct 44

Deployment: *Bon Homme Richard* (CV-31) Jun-Sep 45 F6F-5N

Combat record: 9 victories. Lost 3 pilots on deployment.
Top score: Ens. Philip T. McDonald, 4.

Formed at Charleston, VF(N)-91 rode the brand-new Essex-class carrier *Bon Homme Richard* to WestPac in June 1945. "Bonnie Dick" would become the only aircraft carrier to launch combat missions in three consecutive wars.

Lt.Cdr. Al Minvielle's squadron picked up additional pilots en route to combat, as some VF(N)-53 aviators had been displaced from *Saratoga* when she was mauled off Iwo Jima in February.

Night Fighting 91 claimed two kills and a probable off Japan the evening of 25 July. Ens. Ken Baldwin tagged a Willow trainer while Lt(jg) Bob Klotze splashed a Grace.

The squadron's second intercept came the evening of 9 August. Ens. "JC" Stires, who had claimed a probable on 25 July, definitely splashed a pair of Judys.

Four days later, five kills and a probable, with Ens. Philip T. McDonald accounting for four—two Nicks plus two Frans confirmed and a probable. The other Nick fell to Lt. Robert "Rudder" Kieling.

Remarkable about Fighting 91's success was that all 11 claims occurred during the "witching hour" between 1820 and 1920 on the four days of intercepts.

Wartime CO: Lt.Cdr. Alphonse Minvielle 5 Oct 44

Disestablished: 21 Jun 46

VF-94

Established: 15 Nov 44

Deployment: *Lexington* (CV-16) Jun-Sep 45 F6F-5, -5N, -5P

Combat record: 1 victory. Lost 2 pilots on deployment.

Fighting 94 belonged to the last Navy air group to enter combat in WW II. CVLG-94 was the fifth air group embarked in *Lexington*, but had little chance to match the records of Air Groups 16, 19, or 20. Following a shakedown cruise in June 1945, Lt.Cdr. Bob Morgan's pilots flew a "warmup" strike against Wake Island en route to the fleet anchorage at Leyte. It was a long way from Morgan's operational roots, when he flew with VF-2 and -3 during the 1942 battles. Another notable veteran was George Wrenn, formerly of VF-72.

Sailing for combat in earnest on 1 July, Lex's fighters searched Home Island airspace for airborne targets over the next six weeks. Off Japan 13 August a VF-94 division bagged a Jill at 1626, but identity of the pilots was not stated in the records. It was one of 20 victories that day — two days before the end of hostilities.

Wartime CO: Lt.Cdr. Robert J. Morgan 15 Nov 44

Disestablished: 7 Nov 45

VBF-94

Established: 2 Jan 45

Deployment: *Lexington* (CV-16) Jun-Aug 45 F4U-4

Combat record: No victories. Lost 11 pilots on deployment.

Air Group 94 was still at NAS Atlantic City when Lt.Cdr. Let Wall's VBF-94 was established in January 1945. In less than two weeks the squadron converted from Hellcats to Corsairs, and took "dash fours" to combat in *Lexington* that summer.

Throughout July and August VBF-94 flew strikes and escorts over Japan without much opportunity to engage airborne bandits. However, losses were significant, with seven pilots missing in action and four more killed in routine operations.

Wartime CO: Lt.Cdr L.S. Wall, Jr.

Disestabished: 7 Nov 45

VBF-94 belonged to *Lexington*'s fifth air group of the war, and demonstrated the routine hazard of embarked operations. In combat only during July and August 1945, CVG-94 claimed just one shootdown, while the fighter-bombers lost seven F4U-4 pilots to flak and one operationally.

VF(N)-101

Chronology: established as VF(N)-75 (1 Apr 43)
redesignated VF(N)-101 (1 Jan 44)

Deployments: *Enterprise* (CV-6) Jan-Jul 44 F4U-2
Intrepid (CV-11) Jan-Feb 44 F4U-2

Combat record: 5 victories. No combat losses.
Top score: Lt(jg) Robert F. Holden, 3.

Lt.Cdr. Richard "Chick" Harmer was an experienced fighter pilot with combat from VF-5 aboard *Saratoga* at Guadalcanal. His detachment of VF(N)-75 was sent to carriers while Gus Widhelm's parent unit went to the Solomons and, on 1 January 1944, Harmer's det became VF(N)-101, split between *Enterprise* and *Intrepid*. Lt. Cecil "Swede" Kullberg led Det 11 in "Evil I."

If there were a less enviable job in carrier aviation, it was not readily apparent: flying "bouncing" Corsairs off carriers—at night. The *Intrepid* det had no success, and went ashore after she was torpedoed at Truk in February.

Nearly all the Big E night flying was done by Harmer and his senior pilot, Lt(jg) Bob Holden. Between them, they claimed five confirmed kills, a probable, and three damaged.

Some of the squadron's best interception work involved no shooting. On the evening of 20 June, Chick Harmer used his airborne radar to meet friendly planes returning from the attack on the Japanese fleet. He then led the strays to TF-58.

Fighting 101's last four claims—all twin-engine bombers—were splashed on the nights of 27 and 28 June.

Wartime CO: Lt.Cdr. Richard E. Harmer 1 Jan 44

Disestablished: 2 Oct 44

***Enterprise*'s VF(N)-101 detachment was also employed in daylight defense of the fleet and night search and rescue operations. Standing: (l. to r.) Ens. Poirer, Ens. Brunson, Lt. Cdr. Dick Harmer, CO, Lt. Orphanides, radar fighter director, and Ens. Rulen. Kneeling: (l. to r.) Lt. (jg) Robert F. Holden, Ens. Kelly and Ens. VonSprecken.**

APPENDIX A

THE SQUADRONS

NONCOMBAT NAVY FIGHTING SQUADRONS

VBF-2
Established 2 Jan 45
Disestablished 9 Nov 45

VBF-4
Established 12 May 45
Redes. VF-1B 15 Nov 46

VBF-7
Established 27 Jan 45
Disestablished 8 Jun 46

VBF-8
Established 2 Jan 45
Disestablished 23 Nov 45

VBF-11
Established 5 Apr 45
Redes. VF-12A 15 Nov 46

VBF-13
Established 3 Jan 45
Disestablished 20 Oct 45

VBF-14
Established 15 Jun 45
Disestablished 14 Jun 46

VBF-15
Established 10 Jan 45
Disestablished 20 Oct 45

VBF-18
Established 25 Jan 45
Redes. VF-8A 15 Nov 46

VBF-19
Established 20 Jan 45
Redes. VF-20B 15 Nov 46

VBF-20
Established 16 Apr 45
Redes. VF-10A 15 Nov 46

VF-36 (I)
From VC-18 15 Aug 43
Redes. VF-18 (II) 7 Mar 44

VF-36 (II)
Established 15 May 44
Disestablished 28 Jan 46

VF-39 (II)
Established 15 Mar 45
Disestablished 10 Sep 45

VF-41 (II)
Established 26 Mar 45
Disestablished 15 Nov 46

VF-42 (II)
Established 19 Jul 45
Disestablished 15 Nov 46

VF-43 (I)
Established 1 Aug 43
Disestablished 8 Nov 43

VF-43 (II)
Established 9 Aug 45
Disestablished 17 Jun 46

VF(N)-43
Established 24 Aug 44
To NFTU 2 Jan 45

VF-52 (I)
Established 1 Sep 43
Disestablished 8 Nov 43

VF-52 (II)
Established 6 Jan 45
Disestablished 25 May 45

VF(N)-52
Established 20 Oct 44
Disestablished 15 Dec 45

VF(N)-55
Established 1 Mar 45
Disestablished 11 Dec 45

VF-66
Established 1 Jan 45
Disestablished 18 Oct 45

NONCOMBAT NAVY FIGHTING SQUADRONS (Cont'd.)

VF-74A

Established	1 May 45
Redes. VF-74	1 Aug 45

VBF-74A

Established	1 May 45
Redes. VBF-74	1 Aug 45

VF-75

Established	1 Jun 45
Redes. VF-3B	15 Nov 46

VBF-75A

Established	1 Jun 45
Redes. VBF-75	1 Aug 45

VF(N)-79

Established	20 Mar 44
Redes. VF(N)-41	25 Aug 44

VBF-81

Established	13 May 45
Redes. VF-13B	15 Nov 46

VBF-82

Established	20 Aug 45
Redes. VF-17B	15 Nov 46

VBF-84

Established	12 Jul 45
Disestablished	8 Oct 45

VBF-86

Established	14 Jun 44
Disestablished	21 Nov 45

VF-92

Established	1 Dec 44
Disestablished	18 Dec 45

VBF-92

Established	2 Jan 45
Disestablished	18 Dec 45

VF-93

Established	15 Dec 44
Disestablished	30 Apr 46

VBF-93

Estabished	2 Jan 45
Disestablished	30 Apr 46

VF-95

Established	2 Jan 45
Disestablished	31 Oct 45

VBF-95

Established	2 Jan 45
Disestablished	31 Oct 45

VF-97 (RAG)

Established	1 Nov 44
Disestablished	31 Mar 46

VBF-97 (RAG)

Established	2 Jan 45
Disestablished	31 Mar 46

VF-98 (RAG)

Established	28 Aug 44
Redes. VF-21A	15 Nov 46

VBF-98 (RAG)

Established	1 Feb 45
Redes. VF-22A	15 Nov 46

VF-99 (RAG)

Established	15 Jul 44
Disestablished	6 Sep 45

VBF-99 (RAG)

Established	10 Apr 45
Disestablished	6 Sep 45

VF-100 (RAG)

Established	1 Apr 44
Disestablished	20 Feb 46

VBF-100 (RAG)

Established	2 Jan 45
Disestablished	20 Feb 46

VF(N)-102

Established	10 Mar 44
Redes. VF(N)-42	25 Aug 44

VF(N)-103

Established	6 Apr 44
Redes. VF(N)-90	25 Aug 44

VF(N)-104

Established	20 Apr 44
To VF(N)-90	25 Aug 44

NONCOMBAT NAVY FIGHTING SQUADRONS (Cont'd.)

VF(N)-105
Established 5 May 44
To VF(N)-90 25 Aug 44

VF(N)-106
Established 20 May 44
To VF(N)-90 23 Oct 44

VF(N)-107
Established 5 Jun 44
Disestablished 2 Oct 44

VF(N)-108
Established 20 Jun 44
Disestablished 2 Oct 44

VF(N)-109
Established 5 Jul 44
Disestablished 2 Oct 44

VF(N)-110
Established 20 Jul 44
Disestablished 2 Oct 44

VF(N)-111
Established 20 Aug 44
Disestablished 2 Oct 44

VF-150
Established 22 Jan 45
Disestablished 2 Nov 45

VBF-150
Established 22 Jan 45
Disestablished 2 Nov 45

VF-151
Established 12 Feb 45
Disestablished 6 Oct 45

VBF-151
Established 12 Feb 45
Disestablished 6 Oct 45

VF-152
Established 5 Mar 45
Disestablished 21 Sep 45

VBF-152
Established 5 Mar 45
Disestablished 21 Sep 45

VF-153
Established 26 Mar 45
Redes. VF-15A 15 Nov 46

VBF-153
Established 26 Mar 45
Redes. VF-16A 15 Nov 46

XVF-200
Established 15 Jun 45
Disestablished 15 Mar 46

VF-301
Established 3 Jan 44
Disestablished 1 Aug 44

VF-302
Established 15 Jan 44
Disestablished 1 Aug 44

VF-303
Established 1 Mar 44
Disestablished 4 May 44

VF-305
Established 8 Nov 43
Disestablished 1 Aug 44

VF-306
Established 8 Nov 43
Disestablished 1 Aug 44

RAG: replacement air group

TOP TEN NAVY FIGHTER SQUADRONS

VF-17	Solomons (F4U), *Bunker Hill* (F6F)	315
VF-15	*Essex* (F6F)	310
VF-9	*Ranger* (F4F), *Essex, Yorktown* II (F6F)	256.75
VF-2 (II)	*Hornet* II (F6F)	248
VF-10	*Enterprise* (F4F/F6F), *Intrepid* (F4U)	217
VF-18 (II)	*Intrepid* (F6F)	176.50
VF-31	*Cabot, Belleau Wood* (F6F)	165.60
VF-30	*Belleau Wood, Monterey* (F6F)	159.83
VF/VBF-80	*Ticonderoga, Hancock* (F6F)	159.50
VF-20	*Enterprise, Lexington* II (F6F)	158.16

TOP SIX SQUADRONS BY AIRCRAFT TYPE

Grumman F4F Wildcat

Squadron	Base(s)	Victories
VF-5(I)	*Saratoga*, Solomons	79
VGF-11/VF-21	Solomons	69
VF-11	Solomons	55
VF-3(I)	*Lexington* I, *Yorktown* I	50.50
VF-72	*Hornet* I, Solomons	44
VF-10	*Enterprise*	43

Eastern FM-2 Wildcat

VC-27	*Savo Island*	61.50
VF-26	*Santee*	31
VC-81	*Natoma Bay*	21
VOC-1	*Wake Island, Marcus Island*	20
VC-84	*Makin Island*	19
VC-21	*Nassau, Marcus Island*	18

Grumman F6F Hellcat

VF-15	*Essex*	310
VF-9	*Essex, Lexington II, Yorktown II*	250.75
VF-2 (II)	*Hornet II*	248
VF-18(II)	*Intrepid*	176.50
VF-31	*Cabot, Belleau Wood*	165.60
VF-17	*Hornet II*	161

Vought F4U Corsair

VF-17	Solomons	152
VF-84	*Bunker Hill*	92
VBF-83	*Essex*	91
VF-10	*Intrepid*	87
VBF-6 (II)	*Hancock*	17
VBF-10	*Intrepid*	15

SUCCESSFUL NIGHT-FIGHTER SQUADRONS

VF(N)-41 *Independence* (F6F)	46	(20 night)
VF(N)-76 Various CVs (F6F)	37	(10 night)
VF(N)-90 *Enterprise* (F6F)	31	(21 night)
VF(N)-91 *Bon Homme Richard* (F6F)	9	(0 night?)
VF(N)-77 Various CVs (F6F)	8	(8 night)
VF(N)-75 Solomons (F4U)	7	(7 night)
VF(N)-101 *Enterprise* (F4U)	5	(5 night)
VF(N)-78 *Intrepid, Enterprise* (F6F)	2	(0 night)

An estimated 57 of 145 VF(N) victories were scored at night

SQUADRONS SCORING AGAINST TWO OR MORE AXIS POWERS

VOF/VOC-1	8 Germans (F6F) 20 Japanese (FM)
VF-41/4	14 Vichy (F4F) 2 Germans (F4F) 60 Japanese (F6F)
VF-9	6 Vichy (F4F) 251 Japanese (F6F)
VGF/VF-26	4 Vichy (F4F) 42 Japanese (FM)
VGF/VF-29	1 Vichy (F4F) 113 Japanese (F6F)

SQUADRONS WITH MOST ACES

VF-2 (II)	27	
VF-15	26	
VF-17	23	(11 F4U, 12 F6F)
VF-9	20	
VF-31	14	
VF-8(II)	13	
VF-10	13	(1 F4F, 5 F6F, 4 F4U, 1 F4F/F6F, 2 F6F/F4U)
VF-18 (II)	13	

HIGHEST SQUADRON DAILY CLAIMS
(confirmed-probables-damaged)

VF/VBF-80	*Ticonderoga* *	72	16	15	16 Feb 45	Japan
VF-15	*Essex*	68.5	12	1	19 Jun 44	Marianas
VF-2(II)	*Hornet* II	62	9	0	24 Jun 44	Iwo Jima
VF-83	*Essex*	56	0	0	6 Apr 45	Okinawa
VF-9	*Essex*	55	3	1	11 Nov 43	Rabaul
VF-19	*Lexington* II	53.5	2	3	24 Oct 44	Philippines
VF-8 (II)	*Bunker Hill*	50	5	19	12 Oct 44	Formosa
VF-30	*Belleau Wood*	47	1	0	6 Apr 45	Okinawa
VF-16	*Lexington* II	46	5	1	19 Jun 44	Marianas
VF-15	*Essex*	43	4	6	24 Oct 44	Philippines
VF-18 (II)	*Intrepid*	41	6	3	12 Oct 44	Formosa

* Air Group 80 records do not distinguish between VF and VBF claims

HIGHEST TOTAL DAILY CLAIMS
(confirmed-probables-damaged)

19 Jun 44	Marianas	380	55	22
16 Feb 45	Japan	270	53	114
24 Oct 44	Philippines	270	25	31
6 Apr 45	Okinawa	257	7	10
12 Oct 44	Formosa	224	27	53
16 Apr 45	Okinawa	157	4	10
21 Sep 44	Philippines	147	16	33
11 Nov 43	Rabaul	137	10	14
12 Apr 45	Okinawa	144	3	8
15 Oct 44	Philippines	139	17	20
17 Feb 44	Truk Atoll	124	14	12
24 Jun 44	Iwo Jims	116	14	5
4 May 45	Okinawa	105	2	2

Includes claims by all USN single-engine aircraft; excludes Marine Corps units.

APPENDIX B
THE ACES
U.S. NAVY FIGHTER ACES OF WW II (371)

Squadrons are only those in which confirmed victories were scored. VF-2 entries are the second squadron unless noted.

Ens. Benjamin C. Amsden	VF-22	5	
Lt. Alexander L. Anderson	VF-80	5.5	KIFA 5 Jan 46
Lt. Robert H. Anderson	VF-80	8.5	
Lt. Oscar C. Bailey	VF-28	5	
Lt(jg) Douglas Baker	VF-20	16.33	KIA 14 Dec 44
Cdr. Frederick E. Bakutis	VF-20	7.5	
Lt(jg) Henry W. Balsinger	VF-29	5.33	
Lt(jg) John L. Banks	VF-2	8.5	
Lt. Bruce D. Barackman	VF-50	5	
Lt.Cdr. Frederick A. Bardshar	VF-27	7.5	
Lt(jg) James D. Bare	VF-15	6	
Lt. Lloyd G. Barnard	VF-2	8	
Ens. James M. Barnes	VF-83	6	KIFA 2 Jul 45
Lt. John W. Bartol	VF-16	5	
Lt(jg) Hugh N. Batten	VF-83	7	
Ens. Paul H. N. Beaudry	VF-80	5	
Lt.Cdr. Marshall U. Beebe	VF-17	10.5	
Ens. Jack S. Berkheimer	VF(N)-41	7.5	KIA 16 Dec 44
Lt(jg) Norman R. Berree	VF-15	9	
Ens. Richard L. Bertelson	VF-29	5	
Lt(jg) Walter D. Bishop	VF-29	5	KIA 14 Dec 44
Lt.Cdr. John T. Blackburn	VF-17	11	
Lt. William K. Blair	VF-10, 2	5	
Ens. Richard B. Blaydes	VF-2	5	
Ens. Robert L. Blyth	VF-27	6.5	
Lt. Alfred G. Bolduc	VBF-12	5	

Lt. William J. Bonneau	VF-9	8	KIFA 3 Oct 47
Ens. Clarence A. Borley	VF-15	5	
Lt. Gerald F. Boyle	VF-21, 20	5.5	KIFA 31 Oct 44
Lt. Arthur J. Brassfield	VF-42, 3 (I)	6.33	
Cdr. Charles W. Brewer	VF-15	6.5	KIA 19 Jun 44
Lt. Johnnie J. Bridges	VF-6 (I), 7	6.25	
Lt. Mark K. Bright	VF-5 (I), 16	9	KIA 17 Jun 44
Lt(jg) Samuel J. Brocato	VF-83	7	KIFA 9 Jun 60
Lt. Carl A. Brown, Jr.	VF-27	10.5	
Lt. Carland E. Brunmier	VF-44	6	
Lt(jg) James A. Bryce	VF-22	5.25	KIFA 10 Apr 45
Ens. Robert L. Buchanan	VF-29	5	
Lt.Cdr. Paul D. Buie	VF-16	9	
Lt(jg) William E. Burckhalter	VF-16	6	KIA 11 Jun 44
Lt(jg) Franklin N. Burley	VF-18 (II)	7	
Lt. Roy O. Burnett, Jr.	VF-18 (II)	8	
Lt(jg) Howard M. Burriss	VF-17	7.5	KIA 31 Jan 44
Lt. Matthew S. Brynes, Jr.	VF-9 VBF-12	6	
Lt. James B. Cain	VF-45	8	
Lt. Henry A. Carey, Jr.	VF-72, 30	7	
Lt(jg) Robert B. Carlson	VF-40, 30	9	
Lt(jg) Daniel A. Carmichael	VF-2 VBF-12	12	
Lt(jg) George R. Carr	VF-15	11.5	
Lt(jg) Charles H. Carroll	VF-2	6	
Lt(jg) Cyrus J. Chambers	VF-6 (II) 84	5.33	
Lt(jg) Henry K. Champion	VF-9	5	KIA 4 Jan 45
Lt.Cdr. Leonard J. Check	VF-7	10	
Lt. Oscar I. Chenoweth, Jr.	VF-38, 17	8.5	
Lt(jg) Lawrence A. Clark	VF-83	7	
Ens. Robert A. Clark	VF-17	6	
Lt.Cdr. Walter A. Clarke	VF-5 (I) VF-10	7	
Lt. Donald C. Clements	VF-28	5	
Lt. Robert E. Clements	VF-11	5	
Lt. Robert C. Coats	VF-18 (I) 17	9.33	
Lt. Thaddeus T. Coleman, Jr.	VF-6 (II) 83	10	
Cdr. Wilson M. Coleman	VF-13	6	
Cdr. William M. Collins, Jr.	VF-8 (II)	9	
Lt. Edwin S. Conant	VBF-17	7	John F. Perry
Ens. Thomas J. Conroy	VF-27	7	
Lt(jg) W. Edward Copeland	VF-19	6	
Lt(jg) Paul Cordray	VF-17, VBF-10	7	
Lt. Richard L. Cormier	VF/VBF-80	8	
Lt. Richard D. Cowger	VF-17	6	
Lt(jg) Melvin Cozzens	VF-29	6.5	
Lt. Clement M. Craig	VF-22	11.75	
Lt. Donald F. Cronin	VF-8 (II)	6	
Lt(jg) John T. Crosby	VF-18 (I) 17	5.25	
Lt(jg) Daniel G. Cunningham	VF-17	7	
Ens. Kenneth J. Dahms	VF-30	7	
Lt. Merl W. Davenport	VF-17	6.25	
Lt(jg) George H. Davidson	VF-21 VC-27	5.5	
Lt(jg) Clarence E Davies	VF-82	5	
Lt. Robert H. Davis	VF-18 (II)	5.5	
Cdr. William A. Dean, Jr.	VF-2	11	
Lt(jg) John W. Dear, Jr.	VF(N)-76	7	
Lt. Leslie DeCew	VF-9	6	
Lt. Anthony J. Denman	VF-18 (II)	6	
Lt. Reuben H. Denoff	VF-9 VBF-12	5	
Lt. Richard O. Devine	VF-10	8	
Ens. Lawrence A. Dewing	VF-14	5.5	

Lt. Robert A.M. Dibb	VF-3, 6, 18	7	All (I) KIFA 44
Lt. Landis E. Doner	VF-2	8	
Lt(jg) Daniel B. J. Driscoll	VF-31	5	
Ens. Paul E. Drury	VF-27	6.5	
Lt(jg) James E. Duffy	VF-15	5	
Lt.Cdr. George C. Duncan	VF-15	13.5	
Lt(jg) Robert W. Duncan	VF-5 (II)	7	
Lt(jg) Fred L. Dungan	VF(N)-76	7	
Lt(jg) Bernard Dunn	VF-29	5.33	
Lt. Richard T. Eastmond	VF-1	9	
Lt(jg) Byron A. Eberts	VBF-17	6	
Lt. Bert Eckard	VF-9	7	
Lt.Cdr. Willard E. Eder	VF-2(I) 3(I) 29	6.5	
Lt. William C. Edwards	VF-80	7.5	
Lt. Ralph E. Elliott, Jr.	VC-27	9	
Lt(jg) Eric A. Evenson	VF-30	8.25	
Ens. Charles D. Farmer	VF-10	7.25	
Ens. Robert A. Farnsworth, Jr	VF-19	5	
Lt(jg) Robert P. Fash	VF-50	6	
Lt. Alfred J. Fecke	VF-29	7	
Lt. Edward L. Feightner	VF-10, 8 (II)	9	
Lt. Leo M. Ferko	VC-4 VC-20	5	
Lt(jg) Francis M. Fleming	VF-16	7.5	
Lt. Patrick D. Fleming	VF/VBF-80	19	KIFA 16 Feb 56
Ens. Kenneth A. Flinn	VF-15	5	D 24 Jul 45 POW
Lt(jg) Ralph E. Foltz	VF-15	5	
Lt. George Formanek, Jr.	VF-8 (I) 72, 30,	5	KIA 23 Apr 44
Ens. Carl C. Foster	VF-30	8.5	
Ens. Richard E. Fowler, Jr.	VF-15	6.5	
Lt. Marvin J. Franger	VF-9	9	
Lt(jg) John M. Franks, Jr.	VF-9, 12	7	
Lt. Doris C. Freeman	VF-17, 84	9	KIA 11 May 45
Lt(jg) James B. French	VF-9	11	
Lt(jg) Alfred L. Frendberg	VF-16	6	
Lt.Cdr. Harold N. Funk	VF-23, 26	6.5	
Lt(jg) Franklin T. Gabriel	VF-2	8	
Lt(jg) Dwight B. Galt, Jr.	VF-31	5	
Lt(jg) John R. Galvin	VF-8 (II)	7	
Lt. Noel A. M. Gayler	VF-2 (I) 3 (I)	5	
Lt(jg) John T. Gildea	VF-84	7	KIA 11 May 45
Lt. Clement D. Gile	VF-17	8	
Lt. Roy F. Gillespie	VF-30	6	
Lt. Lindley W. Godson	VBF-83	5	
Lt. Donald Gordon	VF-10	5	
Lt(jg) Vernon E. Graham	VF-11	5	
Cdr. James S. Gray	VF-6 (I), 20	6	
Lt. John F. Gray	VF-5 (II)	8.25	KIFA 3 Jun 46
Lt(jg) Lester E. Gray, Jr.	VF-10	5.25	
Lt. Hayden A. Gregory	VF-82	5	
Lt. Richard J. Griffin	VF-2	8	
Lt. Harlan I. Gustafson	VF-8 (II)	6	
Lt. Mayo A. Hadden, Jr.	VF-9	8	
Lt(jg) Louis R. Hamblin	VF-80	6.5	
Lt(jg) Robert M. Hamilton	VF-83	6	
Lt(jg) Eugene R. Hanks	VF-16	6	
Lt. Willis E. Hardy	VF-17	6.5	
Lt. Everett C. Hargreaves	VF-2	8.5	
Lt. Walter R. Harman	VF-10	6	
Lt. Cecil E. Harris	VF-18 (II)	24	
Lt.Cdr. Leroy E. Harris	VF-10, 2	9.25	

Lt(jg) Thomas S. Harris	VF-18 (I), 17	9	
Lt. William H. Harris	VB-17, VF-83	5	KIA 9 Aug 45
Ens. Charles H. Haverland, Jr	VF-20	6.5	
Lt(jg) Arthur R. Hawkins	VF-31	14	Blues 51-54
Lt(jg(Frank R. Hayde	VF-31	6	KIA 15 Jul 44
Lt. Frank C. Hearrell, Jr.	VF-18 (II)	5	
Ens. Horace W. Heath	VF-10	7	KIFA 8 Jul 45
Lt.Cdr. Roger R. Hedrick	VF-17, 84	12	
Lt. Lloyd P. Heinzen	VF-8 (II)	6	KIFA 11 Nov 45
Lt. Paul M. Henderson, Jr.	VF-1	5	KIA 15 Jun 44
Lt. William E. Henry	VF(N)-41	9.5	
Lt. Samuel B. Hibbard	VF-47	7.33	
Lt. Carlos K. Hildebrandt	VF-33	5	
Lt. Harry E. Hill	VF-5 (II)	7	
Lt. Kenneth G. Hippe	VC-3	5	
Ens. John B. Hoag	VF-82	5	
Lt.Cdr. Ronald W. Hoel	VF-8	5	
Lt.Cdr. Herbert N. Houck	VF-9	6	
Lt. Howard R. Hudson	VF-9	5	
Ens. Charles W. Huffman, Jr.	VF-14	7	
Lt(jg) Robert J. Humphrey	VF-17	5.33	KIFA Korea Jun 52
Lt(jg) Robert Hurst	VF-18 (II)	6	
Lt. Bruce D. Jaques	VF-29	5.5	
Lt. Robert H. Jennings, Jr.	VF-72, 82	9.5	KIFA 30 Jun 54
Lt. Hayden M. Jensen	VF-5 (I)	7	
Ens. Delmar K. Johannsen	VBF-12	5	
Lt(jg) Byron M. Johnson	VF-2	8	
Ens. Wallace R. Johnson	VF-15	5	
Lt(jg) John M. Johnston	VBF-17	8	
Lt(jg) James M. Jones	VF-3(II), VBF-3	7	
Ens. Joseph Kaelin	VF-9	5	
Cdr. William R. Kane	VF-10	6	KIFA 6 Feb 57
Lt.Cdr. Leroy W. J. Keith	VF-80	5.5	
Lt(jg) Ira C. Kepford	VF-17	16	
Ens. Robert R. Kidwell, Jr.	VF-45	5	
Lt. Robert A. Kincaid	VBF-83	5	
Ens. William J. Kingston, Jr.	VF-83	6	
Lt(jg) James J. Kinsella	VF-72, 33	5	
Lt(jg) George N. Kirk	VF-8 (II)	7	
Lt. Philip L. Kirkwood	VF-10	12	
Lt. William M. Knight	VF-14	7.5	KIA 5 Nov 44
Ens. William J. Kostik	VBF-17	5	
Lt. Dean S. Laird	VF-4	5.75	
Ens. Kenneth B Lake	VF-2	6	
Lt. William E. Lamb	VF-27	5	Plus 1 in Korea
Lt(jg) William E. Lamoreaux	VF-8 (II)	5	
Lt. Willis G. Laney	VF-84	5	
Lt. Ned W. Langdon	VF-18 (I), 17	5	
Lt. William N. Leonard	VF-42, 3, 11	6	
Lt(jg) John A. Leppla	VS-2, VF-10	5	KIA 26 Oct 42
Ens. Alfred Lerch	VF-10	7	
Lt. Elvin L. Lindsay	VF-19	8	
Lt(jg) Walter A. Lundin	VF-15	6.5	
Lt(jg) Lewin A. Maberry	VF-84	5	
Lt(jg) Charles M. Mallory	VF-18 (II)	10	
AP1/c Lee P. Mankin, Jr.	VF-6 (I), 5 (I)	5	Only enlisted ace
Lt. Armand G. Manson	VF-82	7	
Lt(jg) Albert E Martin	VF-9	5	
Lt. William J. Masoner	VF-11, 19	12	
Lt. William R. Maxwell	VF-51	7	

Lt(jg) Earl May	VF-17	8	KIFA 22 Oct 51
Lt. Richard H. May	VF-32	5	
Ens. Michele A. Mazzocco	VF-30	5	
Cdr. David McCampbell	VF-15	34	Medal of Honor
Lt(jg) Thomas G. McClelland	VF-5 (II)	7.33	
Lt. Edgar B. McClure	VBF-9	5	
Ens. William A. McCormick	VF-50, 8 (II)	7	
Lt. Leo B. McCudden	VF-20	5	
Lt.Cdr. Elbert S. McCuskey	VF-42, 3, 8(II)	13.5	
Lt. Charles E. McGowan	VF-9	6.5	
Ens. Joseph D. McGraw	VC-10, 80	5	
Lt(jg) Donald J. McKinley	VF-25	5	
Ens. Donald M. McPherson	VF-83	5	
Lt. Hamilton McWhorter III	VF-9, 12	12	
Lt.Cdr. Roger W. Mehle	VF-6 (I), 28	5.66	
Lt. Louis A. Menard	VF-9,VBF-12	9	
Lt. Adolph Mencin	VF-31	6	
LtCdr Frederick H. Michaelis	VF-12	5	
Ens. Johnnie G. Miller	VF-30	8	
Lt. Charles B. Milton	VF-15	5	
Lt(jg) Robert Mims	VF-17	6	
Lt(jg) Harris E. Mitchell	VF-9	10	
Lt(jg) Henry E. Mitchell, Jr.	VBF-17	6	KIA 3 Apr 45
Lt(jg) Norman W. Mollard, Jr.	VF-45	6	
Ens. Arthur P. Mollenhauer	VF-18 (II)	5	KIA 29 Oct 44
Lt(jg) John R. Montapert	VF-44	6	
Lt(jg) H. Blake Moranville	VF-11	6	POW 12 Jan 45
Lt. Bert D. Morris, Jr.	VF-15	7	
Lt. William C. Moseley	VF-1	5	KIA 4 Jul 44
Lt. Douglas W. Mulcahy	VF-31	8	
Lt(jg) Robert E. Murray	VF-29	10.33	
Lt. Robert J. Nelson	VF-5 (II)	7	
Ens. Robert K. Nelson	VF-20	6.66	KIA 19 Nov 44
Lt(jg) Myrvin E. Noble	VF-2	7	
Lt. Cornelius N. Nooy	VF-31	19	
Lt. Cleveland L. Null	VF-16	7	KIFA 9 Oct 52
Lt.Cdr. Edward H. O'Hare	VF-3(I), 6(II)	7	KIA 26 Nov 43
Ens. Austin L. Olsen	VF-30	5	
Ens. Paul O'Mara, Jr.	VF-19	7	
Ens. John Orth	VF-9	6	
Lt.Cdr. Eddie C. Outlaw	VF-32	6	
Lt. Edward W. Overton, Jr.	VF-15	5	
Lt.Cdr. Edward M. Owen	VF-5 (II)	5	
Ens. Elbert W. Parrish	VF-80	6	
Lt. John J. Paskoski	VF-19	6	250
Lt. James L. Pearce	VF-18 (I), 17	5.25	
Ens. David P. Philips, III	VF-30	5	
Ens. Edward A. Phillips	VF-20	5	
Lt. Harvey P. Picken	VF-18 (II)	11	
Ens. George W. Pigman, Jr.	VF-15	8.5	
Ens. Claude W. Plant	VF-15	8.5	KIA 12 Sep 44
Lt(jg) Tilman E. Pool	VF-17	6	
Ens. Albert J. Pope	VF-13	7	
Lt(jg) Ralston M. Pound, Jr.	VF-16	6	
Lt(jg) Luther D. Prater, Jr.	VF-19	8.5	
Lt(jg) Melvin M. Prichard	VF-20	5.25	
Ens. Norwald R. Quiel	VF-10	6	
Ens. James V. Reber, Jr.	VF-30	11	
Lt(jg) Eugene D. Redmond	VF-10, 2	9.25	KIFA 3 Jun 51
Lt(jg) Francis R. Register	VF-6 (I), 5 (I)	7	KIFA 16 May 43

Lt(jg) Daniel R. Rehm, Jr.	VF-50, 8 (II)	9	
Lt. Thomas H. Reidy	VBF-83	10	
Lt. Russell L. Reiserer	VF-10, VF(N)-76	9	
Lt. Thomas J. Rennemo	VF-18 (II)	6	
Lt(jg) Joseph E. Reulet	VF-10	5	
Lt. Glenn M. Revel	VF-14	5.75	
Lt(jg) Vincent A. Rieger	VF-31	5	
Lt.Cdr. James F. Rigg	VF-15	11	
Lt. Thomas D. Roach	VF-21	5.5	KIA 25 Jul 43
Lt. Joe D. Robbins	VF-6 (II), 85	5	
Ens. Leroy W. Robinson	VF-2	5	
Ens. Ross F. Robinson	VF-2	5	
Lt(jg) Ralph J. Rosen	VF-8 (II)	6	
Lt. Herman J. Rossi, Jr.	VF-19	6	
Lt(jg) Donald E. Runyon	VF-6(I) 18(I)	11	
Lt(jg) Roy W. Rushing	VF-15	13	
Lt(jg) John J. Sargent, Jr.	VF-18 (I), 84	5.25	KIA 11 May 45
Lt. Jimmie E. Savage	VF-11	7	
Lt. Henry H. Scales	VF-31	6.20	
Cdr. Gordon E. Schecter	VF-45	5	KIA 18 Mar 45
Lt. John L. Schell	VF-3 (II)	5	
Lt(jg) James E. Schiller	VF-5 (II)	5	
Ens. Frank E. Schneider	VF-33	7	KIA 9 Jan 44
Lt. Albert Seckel, Jr.	VF-19	6	
Ens. Larry R. Self	VF-15	8.5	
Lt(jg) Robert W. Shackford	VF-2	5	
Lt(jg) Hugh V. Sherrill	VF-81	5.5	
Lt. James A. Shirley	VF-27	12.5	
Lt.Cdr. Sam L. Silber	VF-27, 18(I)	7	
Lt(jg) Arthur Singer, Jr.	VF-15	10	
Lt(jg) Lester H. Sipes	VF-10, 2	5	
Lt(jg) Frank Sistrunk	VF-17	5	KIA 3 Sep 51 Korea
Lt(jg) Warren A. Skon	VF-2	7	
Lt(jg) Albert C. Slack	VF-19	6.5	
Lt. Armistead B. Smith, Jr.	VF-9, VBF-12	10	
Lt(jg) Clinton L. Smith	VF-9	6	
Cdr. Daniel F. Smith, Jr.	VF-20	6.083	
Lt(jg) John M. Smith	VF-17, 84	10	
Lt. Kenneth D. Smith	VF(N)-90, 82	5	KIFA 19 Apr 55
Ens. Nicholas J. Smith III	VF-13	6	
Lt(jg) Irl V Sonner	VF-29	5	KIFA 22 Mar 45
Cdr. James J. Southerland	VF-5 (I), 83, 23	5	KIFA 12 Oct 49
Lt(jg) Clyde P. Spitler	VF-2	5	
Lt. Richard E. Stambook	VF-27	10	
Ens. Gordon A. Stanley	VF-27	8	
Lt(jg) Carlton B. Starkes	VF-5 (I)	6	
Lt. James S. Stewart	VF-31	10	
Lt. Charles R. Stimpson	VF-11	16	
Lt(jg) John D. Stokes	VF-14	6.5	
Lt(jg) Carl V. Stone	VBF-17	5	KIFA 13 Mar 67
Lt. John R. Strane	VF-15	13	
Lt.Cdr. Johnnie C. Strange	VF-50	5	
Lt(jg) Frederick J. Streig	VF-17	5	
Lt(jg) Harvey W. Sturdevant	VF-30	6	
Lt(jg) Harry W. Swinburne, Jr	VF-45	5	
Lt. James S. Swope	VF-11	9.66	
Lt(jg) John C. C. Symmes	VF-21, 15	11	
Lt(jg) Ray A. Taylor, Jr.	VF-14	6.5	
Lt. Will W Taylor	VF-41/4	6	
Lt.Cdr. John S. Thach	VF-3	6	

Lt(jg) Robert H. Thelen	VF-24	6	
Lt. Robert F. Thomas	VF-21	5.25	
Lt(jg) Edward W. Toaspern	VF-31, 18 (I)	7	KIFA 15 Oct 50
Lt(jg) John W. Topliff	VF-8 (II)	5	
Lt. Ross E. Torkelson	VGF-11, VF-21	6	KIA 22 Jul 43
Lt(jg) Eugene P. Townsend	VF-27	5	KIFA 14 Dec 53
Lt. Frederick W. Tracey	VF-18 (II)	5	
Ens. Franklin W. Troup	VF-29	7	
Ens. Myron M. Truax	VF-83	7	
Lt. Charles H. Turner	VF-31	6	
Lt. Edward B. Turner	VF-14	7	
Lt(jg) Wendell V. Twelves	VF-15	13	
Lt(jg) Vernon R. Ude	VF-10	5	
Lt. Donald E. Umphres	VF-83	6	KIFA 4 Jun 47
Lt. Eugene A. Valencia	VF-9	23	
Lt(jg) Peter J. VanDerLinden	VF-5	6	
Lt. Rudolph D. Van Dyke, Jr.	VF-18 (II)	5	
Lt. Arthur Van Haren, Jr.	VF-2	9	
Lt. Stanley W. Vejtasa	VS-5, VF-10	10.25	
Lt. Merriwell W. Vineyard	VF-2	6	
Lt. Harold E. Vita	VF-9, 12	6	
Lt. Roy M. Voris	VF-2	7	Blue Angels '46
Lt.Cdr. Albert O. Vorse, Jr.	VF-3, 2, 6, 80	11.5	All (I) squadrons
Lt. Alexander Vraciu	VF-6 (II)	16 19	
Ens. Lyttleton T. Ward	VF-83	5	
Lt(jg) Jack O. Watson	VF-33	5	
Lt(jg) Charles E. Watts	VF-18 (I), 17	8.75	
Ens. Wilbur B. Webb	VF-2	7	
Lt. John M. Wesolowski	VF-5 (I), VBF-9	7	
Lt(jg) Robert G. West	VF-14	5	
Lt. Henry S. White	VF-11	5	
Lt. Bruce W. Williams	VF-19	7	
Lt(jg) Robert C. Wilson	VF-31	7	
Lt. Murray Winfield	VF-17	6	
Cdr. T. Hugh Winters	VF-19	8	
Lt. John L. Wirth	VF-31	14	KIFA 13 Apr 45
Lt(jg) John T. Wolf	VF-2	7	
Ens. Walter A Wood	VF-20	5.5	KIA 18 Oct 44
Lt. Millard J. Wooley	VF-18 (I), 17	5	
Lt(jg) Robert C. Woolverton	VF-45	6	KIFA date?
Cdr. Malcolm T. Wordell	VF-44	7	
Ens. George L. Wrenn	VF-72	5.25	
Ens. Harold Yeremian	VBF-17	6	KIFA 13 Aug 51
Lt(jg) Earling W. Zaeske	VF-2	5	
Lt. John A. Zink	VF-11, 18, 7	5	

THE TOP 50 NAVY ACES

Cdr. David McCampbell	VF-15	34	Medal of Honor
Lt. Cecil E. Harris	VF-27, 18 (II)	23	22 in VF-18
Lt. Eugene A. Valencia	VF-9	23	
Lt. Patrick D. Fleming	VF/VBF-80	19	10 in VF-80
Lt. Cornelius Nooy	VF-31	19	
Lt. Alexander Vraciu	VF-6, 16, 20	19	10 in VF-16
Lt(jg) Douglas Baker	VF-20	16.33	KIA 14 Dec 44
Lt(jg) Ira Kepford	VF-17	16	
Lt. Charles R. Stimpson	VF-11	16	
Lt(jg) Arthur R. Hawkins	VF-31	14	
Lt. John L. Wirth	VF-31	14	11th

Lt.Cdr. George C. Duncan	VF-15	13.50	
Lt.Cdr. Elbert S. McCuskey	VF-42, 3, 8(II)	13.50	7 in VF-8
Lt(jg) Roy W. Rushing	VF-15	13	
Lt. John R. Strane	VF-15	13	
Lt(jg) Wendell V. Twelves	VF-15	13	
Lt. James A. Shirley	VF-27	12.50	
Lt. Daniel A. Carmichael	VF-2 VBF-12	12	8 in VF-2
Lt.Cdr. Roger R. Hedrick	VF-17, 84	12	9 in VF-17
Lt(jg) Philip L. Kirkwood	VF-10	12	20th
Lt. William J. Masoner	VF-11, 19	12	10 in VF-19
Lt.Cdr. Hamilton McWhorter	VF-9, VF-12	12	10 in VF-9
Lt. Clement M. Craig	VF-22	11.75	
Lt. George R. Carr	VF-15	11.50	
Lt.Cdr. Albert O. Vorse	VF-2, 3, 6, 80	11.50	6 in VF-80
Cdr. Frederick E. Bakutis	VF-20	11	
Lt.Cdr. John T. Blackburn	VF-17	11	
Cdr. William A. Dean, Jr.	VF-2 (II)	11	
Lt(jg) James B. French	VF-9	11	
Lt.Cdr. Charles M. Mallory	VF-18 (II)	11	30th
Lt. Harvey P. Picken	VF-18 (II)	11	
Lt(jg) James V. Reber, Jr.	VF-30	11	
Lt.Cdr. James F. Rigg	VF-15	11	
Lt. Richard E Stambook	VF-27	11	
Lt(jg) John C.C. Symmes	VF-21, 15	11	5.5 in each
Lt(jg) Donald E. Runyon	VF-6, 18 (I)	11	8 in VF-6
Lt.Cdr. Marshall U. Beebe	VF-17	10.50	37th
Lt. Carl A. Brown, Jr.	VF-27	10.50	
Lt. Robert E. Murray	VF-29	10.33	
Lt. Stanley W. Vejtasa	VS-5 VF-10	10.25	3 in VS-5
Lt. Robert H. Anderson	VF-80	10	
Lt.Cdr. Leonard J. Check	VF-7	10	KIA 4 Jan 45
Lt.Cdr. Thaddeus T. Coleman	VF-6 VF-83	10	8 in VF-83
Lt(jg) Harris E. Mitchell	VF-9	10	
Lt. Thomas H. Reidy	VBF-83	10	
Lt(jg) Arthur R. Singer	VF-15	10	
Lt. Armistead B. Smith, Jr.	VF-9 VBF-12	10	6 in VF-9
Lt(jg) John M. Smith	VF-17, 84	10	7 in VF-84
Lt. James S. Stewart	VF-31	10	
Lt. James S. Swope	VF-11	9.66	

TOP NAVY ACES BY AIRCRAFT TYPE

Grumman F4F Wildcat (21 aces)

Mach. Donald E. Runyon	VF-6	*Enterprise*	8+3 F6F
Lt. Stanley W. Vejtasa	VF-10	*Enterprise*	7.25
Ens. Hayden M. Jensen	VF-5	*Saratoga*, Guadalcanal	7
Lt(jg) Francis R. Register	VF-6, 5	*Enterprise*, Guadalcanal	7
Lt(jg) Elbert S. McCuskey	VF-42, 3	*Yorktown* I	6.50 +7 F6F
Lt. Arthur J. Brassfield	VF-42, 3	*Yorktown* I	6.33

Eastern FM-2 Wildcat (5 aces)

Lt. Ralph E. Elliot	VC-27	*Savo Island*	9
Lt. Cdr. Harold N. Funk	VF-26	*Santee*	6
Lt. Leo M. Ferko	VC-4, 20	*White Plains, Marcus Island*	5
Lt. Kenneth G. Hippe	VC-3	*Kalinin Bay*	5
Ens. Joseph D. McGraw	VC-10, 80	*Gambier Bay, Manila Bay*	5

Grumman F6F Hellcat	(306 aces)		
Cdr. David McCampbell	CAG-15	*Essex*	34
Lt. Eugene A. Valencia	VF-9	*Essex, Lex II, York II*	23
Lt. Cecil E. Harris	VF-18	*Intrepid*	22 +1 F4F
Lt. Patrick D. Fleming	VF-80	*Ticonderoga, Hancock*	19
Lt. Cornelius Nooy	VF-31	*Cabot, Belleau Wood*	19
Lt. Alexander Vraciu	VF-6, 16	*Independence, Lex II*	19

Vought F4U Corsair	(24 aces)		
Lt(jg) Ira C. Kepford	VF-17	Solomons	16
Lt.Cdr. Roger R. Hedrick	VF-17, 84	Solomons, *Bunker Hill*	12
Lt.Cdr. Tom Blackburn	VF-17	Solomons	11
Lt.Cdr. Thomas H. Reidy	VBF-83	*Essex*	10
Lt. John M. Smith	VF-17, 84	Solomons, *Bunker Hill*	10

Aces in Two Aircraft

Lt.Cdr. Elbert S. McCuskey	VF-42, 3, 8 (II)	6.5 F4F	7 F6F
Lt. Charles R. Stimpson	VF-11	6 F4F	10 F6F
Lt(jg) John C. Symmes	VF-21, 15	5.5 F4F	5.5 F6F
Lt.Cdr. Albert O. Vorse	VF-2, 3, 6, 80	5.5 F4F	6 F6F

Total Aces by Aircraft Type

F6F	306 *	
F4U	24	
F4F	21 *	
FM	5	
F4F/F6F	10	
F6F/F4U	5	
F4F/F4U	1	(W.E. Clarke, 4 F4F/3 F4U)
F4F/FM	1	(G.H. Davidson, .5 F4F/4.5 FM)
SBD/F4F	1	(J.A. Leppla, 4 SBD/1 F4F)
SB2C/F6F	1	(W.H. Harris, 1 SB2C/4 F6F)
Total	375 (371 actual) *	

* Figures don't conform, as 4 pilots were aces both in F4F and F6F.

THE LEADING NAVY ACE

Lt(jg) Edward H. O'Hare	VF-3	F4F	5	20 Feb 42
Lt(jg) Elbert S. McCuskey	VF-3	F4F	6.5	4 Jun 42
Mach. Donald Runyon	VF-6	F4F	8	24 Aug 42
Lt(jg) Ira C. Kepford	VF-17	F4U	10	29 Jan 44
Lt(jg) Ira C. Kepford	VF-17	F4U	16	19 Feb 44
Lt(jg) Alexander Vraciu	VF-16	F6F	18	19 Jun 44
Lt(jg) Alexander Vraciu	VF-16	F6F	19	20 Jun 44
Cdr. David McCampbell	VF-15	F6F	19	24 Sep 44
Cdr. David McCampbell	VF-15	F6F	20	21 Oct 44
Cdr. David McCampbell	VF-15	F6F	34	14 Nov 44

First double ace: Lt(jg) Donald E. Runyon, VF-8 (VF-6), 4 Jan 44
First triple ace: Lt(jg) Ira Kepford, VF-17, 19 Feb 44
First quadruple ace: Cdr. David McCampbell, CVG-15, 21 Oct 44

THE FIRST TWENTY NAVY ACES

Name and rank	Unit	(prior)	Date No. 5	Total
Lt(jg) Edward H. O'Hare +	VF-3		20 Feb 42	7
Lt. Noel A.M. Gayler	VF-2	(VF-3)	8 May 42	5
Lt(jg) Arthur J. Brassfield	VF-3	(VF-42)	4 Jun 42	6.33
Lt(jg) Elbert S. McCuskey	VF-3	(VF-42)	4 Jun 42	13.50
Lt.Cdr. John S. Thach	VF-3		4 Jun 42	6.50
Lt. Hayden M. Jensen	VF-5		24 Aug 42	7
Mach. Donald E. Runyon	VF-6		24 Aug 42	11
Lt(jg) Carlton B. Starkes	VF-5		24 Aug 42	6
Lt. Albert O. Vorse, Jr.	VF-6		24 Aug 42	11.50
AP1/c Lee P. Mankin, Jr.	VF-5	(VF-6)	27 Sep 42	5
Lt(jg) Francis R. Register +	VF-5	(VF-5)	27 Sep 42	7
Ens. John M. Wesolowski	VF-5		28 Sep 42	7
Ens. Mark K. Brigh +	VF-5		29 Sep 42	9
Lt(jg) John A. Leppla +	VF-10	(VS-2)	26 Oct 42	5
Lt. Stanley W. Vejtasa	VF-10	(VS-5)	26 Oct 42	10.25
Ens. George L. Wrenn	VF-72		26 Oct 42	5.25
Lt(jg) Vernon E. Graham	VF-11		12 Jun 43	5
Lt. William N. Leonard	VF-11	(VF-42/3)	12 Jun 43	6
Lt(jg) Charles R. Stimpson	VF-11		6 Jul 43	16
Lt. Ross E. Torkelson +	VF-21		13 Jul 43	6

+ Killed in line of duty

ACES IN A DAY (55)

Name and Rank	Unit	Date	E/A	Total	Comment
Lt(jg) E.H. O'Hare	VF-3	20 Feb 42	5	7	MOH, KIA
Lt(jg) E.S. McCuskey	VF-3	4 Jun 42	5	13.50	
Lt. S.W. Vejtasa	VF-10	26 Oct 42	7	10.25	
Ens. G.W. Wrenn	VF-72	26 Oct 42	5	5.25	
Lt. V.E. Graham	VF-11	12 Jun 43	5	5	
Lt(jg) E.R. Hanks	VF-16	23 Nov 43	5	6	
Lt.Cdr. E.C. Outlaw	VF-32	29 Apr 44	5	6	
Lt. L.G. Barnard	VF-2	15 Jun 44	5	8	
Cdr. D. McCampbell	VF-15	19 Jun 44	5+2	34	1st time
Lt(jg) A. Vraciu	VF-16	19 Jun 44	6	18	
Ens. W.W. Webb	VF-2	19 Jun 44	6	7	
Lt(jg) G.R. Carr	VF-15	19 Jun 44	5	11.50	
Lt. R.L. Reiserer	VF(N)-76	19 Jun 44	5	9	
Cdr. C.W. Brewer	VF-15	19 Jun 44	4+1	6.50	KIA
Lt(jg) E.C. Hargreaves	VF-2	24 Jun 44	4+1	8.50	
Lt.Cdr. J.F. Rigg	VF-15	9 Sep 44	5	11	
Lt(jg) A.R. Hawkins	VF-31	13 Sep 44	5	14	
Lt(jg) C.M. Mallory	VF-18	21 Sep 44	3+2	10	
Lt. H.P. Picken	VF-18	21 Sep 44	4+1	11	
Lt(jg) C.N. Nooy	VF-31	21 Sep 44	5	19	
Cdr. W.M. Collins Jr.	VF-8	12 Oct 44	5	9	
Ens. A.P. Mollenhauer	VF-18	12 Oct 44	5	5	KIA
Lt. C.R. Stimpson	VF-11	14 Oct 44	5	16	
Lt. A.J. Fecke	VF-29	16 Oct 44	5	7	
Ens. R.L. Buchanan	VF-29	16 Oct 44	5	5	
Lt. E.B. Turner	VF-14	18 Oct 44	5	7	
Cdr. D. McCampbell	VF-15	24 Oct 44	9	34	2nd, MOH
Lt(jg) R.W. Rushing	VF-15	24 Oct 44	6	13	

ACES IN A DAY (55) [Cont'd.]

Name and Rank	Unit	Date	E/A	Total	Comment
Lt(jg) W.J. Masoner	VF-19	24 Oct 44	6	12	
Ens. T.J. Conroy	VF-27	24 Oct 44	6	7	
Lt. C.A. Brown, Jr.	VF-27	24 Oct 44	5	10	
Lt. J.A. Shirley	VF-27	24 Oct 44	5	12.50	
Lt(jg) E.P. Townsend	VF-27	24 Oct 44	5	5	
Lt.Cdr. H.N. Funk	VF-26	24 Oct 44	5+1	6.50	
Lt. K.G. Hippe	VC-3	24 Oct 44	5	5	
Lt. R.H. Anderson	VF-80	14 Dec 44	5	8.50	
Lt. C.M. Craig	VF-22	21 Jan 45	5	11.75	
Lt. A.L. Anderson	VF-80	16 Feb 45	5	8.50	
Lt. W.C. Edwards, Jr.	VF-80	16 Feb 45	5	7.50	
Lt. P.D. Fleming	VF-80	16 Feb 45	5	19	
Lt.Cdr. L.W. Keith	VF-80	16 Feb 45	5	5.50	
Cdr. G.E. Schecter	VF-45	16 Feb 45	4+1	5	KIA
Ens. R.R. Kidwell	VF-45	16 Feb 45	3+2	5	
Lt.Cdr. M.U. Beebe	VF-17	18 Mar 45	5	10.50	
Lt. R.C. Coats	VF-17	18 Mar 45	5	9	
Lt(jg) H.E. Mitchell	VBF-17	21 Mar 45	5	6	
Ens. C.C. Foster	VF-30	6 Apr 45	6	8.50	
Ens. K.J. Dahms	VF-30	6 Apr 45	5.50	7	
Ens. J.G. Miller	VF-30	6 Apr 45	5	8	
Lt(jg) W.E. Hardy	VF-17	6 Apr 45	5	7	
Ens. A. Lerch	VF-10	16 Apr 45	7	7	
Lt(jg) P.L. Kirkwood	VF-10	16 Apr 45	6	12	
Lt. E.A. Valencia	VF-9	17 Apr 45	6	23	
Lt. J.T. Crosby	VF-17	26 Apr 45	5	5.25	
Ens. M.M. Truax	VF-83	4 May 45	6	7	
Lt. B. Eckard	VF-9	11 May 45	5	7	

3+2 = three victories in first sortie, two in the second
MOH = Medal of Honor
KIA = Killed in Action (see KIA list for details)

5 F4F
1 FM
47 F6F (McCampbell twice)
2 F4U

55 total

NAVY ACES KILLED IN ACTION (KIA) OR IN FLYING ACCIDENTS (KIFA)

Lt(jg) John A. Leppla	(age 26)	VF-10	KIA 26 Oct 42
Lt. Francis R. Register	(25)	(VF-6, 5)	KIFA 16 May 43
Lt(jg) Thomas D. Roach	(24)	VF-21	KIA 25 Jul 43
Lt. Ross E. Torkelson	(29)	VF-21	KIA 27 Jul 43
Lt. Cdr. Edward H. O'Hare	(29)	CAG-6	KIA 26 Nov 43
Lt. George Formanek, Jr.	(24)	VF-30	KIA 23 Apr 44
Ens. Frank E. Schneider	(23)	VF-33	KIA 9 Jan 44
Lt(jg) Howard W. Burriss	(22)	VF-17	KIA 31 Jan 44
Lt(jg) William E. Burckhalter	(22)	VF-16	KIA 11 Jun 44
Lt. Paul M. Henderson, Jr.	(27)	VF-1	KIA 15 Jun 44
Lt. Mark K. Bright	(25)	VF-16	KIA 17 Jun 44
Cdr. Charles W. Brewer	(33)	VF-15	KIA 19 Jun 44

NAVY ACES KILLED IN ACTION (KIA) OR IN FLYING ACCIDENTS (KIFA)[Cont'd.]

Lt. William C. Moseley	(27)	VF-1	KIA 4 Jul 44
Lt(jg) Frank R. Hayde	(23)	VF-31	KIA 15 Jul 44
Lt. Robert A.M. Dibb	(23)	(VF-3, 6, 18)	KIFA 29 Aug 44
Lt. Claude W. Plant	(24)	VF-15	KIA 12 Sep 44
Ens. Walter A. Wood	(23)	VF-20	KIA 18 Oct 44
Lt(jg) Gerald F. Boyle	(27)	VF-20	KIFA 31 Oct 44
Lt. William M. Knight	(25)	VF-14	KIA 5 Nov 44
Ens. Robert K. Nelson	(21)	VF-20	KIA 19 Nov 44
Ens. Jack Berkheimer	(20)	VFN-41	KIA 6 Dec 44
Lt(jg) Douglas Baker	(23)	VF-20	KIA 14 Dec 44
Lt(jg) Walter D. Bishop	(24)	VF-29	KIA 14 Dec 44
Lt.Cdr. Leonard J. Check	(33)	VF-7	KIA 4 Jan 45
Cdr. Gordon E. Schecter	(32)	VF-45	KIA 18 Mar 45
Lt(jg) Irl V. Sonner	(25)	VF-29	KIFA 22 Mar 45
Lt(jg) James A. Bryce	(23)	VF-22	KIFA 10 Apr 45
Lt. John L. Wirth	(27)	(VF-31)	KIFA 13 Apr 45
Lt. Doris C. Freeman	(25)	VF-84	KIA 11 May 45
Lt(jg) John T. Gildea	(24)	VF-84	KIA 11 May 45
Lt. John J. Sargent	(25)	VF-84	KIA 11 May 45
Ens. James M. Barnes	(21)	VF-83	KIFA 2 Jul 45
Ens. Horace W. Heath	(23)	VF-10	KIFA 8 Jul 45
Lt(jg) J. A. Flinn	(21)	(VF-15)	Died 24 Jul 45*
Lt. William H. Harris, Jr.	(26)	VBF-83	KIA 9 Aug 45

(VF-31) indicates that the ace was no longer with his squadron at the time of death. KIA may indicate that cause of death was combat-related rather than by direct enemy action.

* Flinn, shot down 13 Oct 44, died in captivity in Japan.

These 35 aces were aged 20 to 33. The median was 24.

NAVAL ACADEMY ACES

Name	Victories	USNA	Comments
Frederick E. Bakutis	7	1935	
Frederick A. Bardshar	8	1938	
John T. Blackburn	11	1933	
Charles W. Brewer	6.5	1934	KIA Jun 1944
Paul D. Buie	9	1933	
Robert E. Clements	5	1940	
Thaddeus T. Coleman	6	1934	
William M. Collins	9	1934	
William A. Dean	11	1934	
George C. Duncan	13.5	1939	
James H. Flatley	4 to 6.5	1929	
Patrick D. Fleming	19	1941	
Noel A.M. Gayler	5	1935	
James S. Gray	6	1936	
Leroy E. Harris	12	1939	
William R. Kane	6	1933	
William E. Lamb	5	1940	Plus 1 in Korea
William N. Leonard	6	1938	
David McCampbell	34	1933	MOH
Roger W. Mehle	5.66	1937	
Frederick H. Michaelis	5	1940	
Edward H. O'Hare	7	1937	KIA Nov 43; MOH
Edward C. Outlaw	6	1935	
Gordon E. Schecter	5	1935	KIA Mar 45

NAVAL ACADEMY ACES (Cont'd.)

Daniel F. Smith	6	1932
James J. Southerland	5	1936
John S. Thach	6	1927
Albert O. Vorse	11.5	1937
T. Hugh Winters	8	1935
Malcolm T. Wordell	7	1935

1927	1	1934	4	1938	2
1929	1	1935	6	1939	2
1932	1	1936	2	1940	3
1933	4	1937	3	1941	1

Of these 30 aviators, 15 commanded air groups during the war and 8 more became combat squadron commanders. Collectively, they were credited with 430.66 victories for an average of nearly 15—twice the norm for American aces. Ten made flag rank, of whom Gayler, Michaelis, and Thach retired as four-star admirals. By way of comparison, 12 West Point graduates became aces in WW II or Korea.

FIGHTER ACE MISCELLANY

What were the odds?

Some 536 aviators were credited with four or more aerial victories, of whom 371 became aces. Therefore, a Navy fighter pilot with four kills had a 69% chance of "making ace." The remaining 166 broke down thusly:

4.83	4 pilots
4.50	27 pilots
4.33	4 pilots
4.25	3 pilots
4.16	1 pilot
4.14	1 pilot
4.08	1 pilot
4.00	125 pilots

Oldest ace: Lt.Cdr. John S. Thach, VF-3, 37:1:15 on 4 June 42

Youngest ace: Ens. Jack Berkheimer, VF(N)-41, 20:2:24 on 24 0ct 1944.

Ensigns: at least 63 ensigns became aces. Highest scoring was VF-20's Doug Baker, with 12 kills before promotion to Lt(jg).

Only noncommissioned ace: AP1/c Lee Paul Mankin, VF-5 and -6.

Only ace to score against Germany and Japan: Lt. Dean S. Laird, VF-4, 5.75 total.

Top scorers against Western Axis (Germany and Vichy)

Lt(jg) Bruce N. Mayhew	VF-41/4	2.75	2.75 total
Lt(jg) Charles V. August	VF-41	2	4.50 total
Lt. Maynard M. Furney	VF-41	2	2 total
Lt(jg) Edward W. Olszewski	VOF-1	2	3 total
Lt.Cdr. John Raby	VF-9	2	2 total
Lt(jg) Charles A. Shields	VF-41	2	3 total
Lt. Ernest W. Wood, Jr.	VF-41	2	2 total

Only ace to score on three consecutive tours: Lt. Marvin J. Franger, VF-9; nine victories.

Top land-based ace: Lt(jg) Ira Kepford, VF-17, 16 victories.

Last Navy aces: Lts. John W. Bartol and Cleveland L. Null (VF-16), and Lt. William H. Harris, Jr. (VBF-83). All on 28 July 1945.

Killed in the Korean War: Eugene D. Redmond, ex VF-10 and -2 (KIFA 3 Jun 51); Frank Sistrunk, ex VF-17 (KIA 3 Sep 51); and R.J. Humphrey, ex VF-17 (KIFA 15 Jun 52).

COMBINED ARMS

At least two naval aviators scored their first victories in the service of foreign nations.

Lt. Hollis Hills of VF-32 claimed four victories in Hellcats while flying from *Langley* in 1944. However, his first success was achieved over Dieppe on 19 August 1942, flying a Mustang I of No. 414 Squadron, Royal Canadian Air Force. It was also the first of some 5,500 Mustang victories over the next three years.

Lt.Cdr. Fritz E. Wolf of VBF-3 aboard *Yorktown* claimed a Tony over Tokyo on 16 February 1945. His first four claims were made while flying P-40s with the American Volunteer Group in China during 1941-42.

Neither pilot is strictly a Navy ace, but both have rare status within the ranks of American fighter aces.

CONFIRMATION PENDING

At some point, the following pilots were credited with five or more victories. Olynyk's exhaustive research has revealed that, in some cases, fractions were counted as whole credits, either from confusion or by rounding up, or official records gave higher totals without supporting details. Undoubtedly some of these pilots did shoot down five enemy aircraft.

Ens. Fred F. Ackerman	VF-80	4.5	(5)
Lt. James D. Billo	VF-10, 18 (I)	3.25	(5)
Lt. John W. Fair	VF-80	4+	(6)
Lt.Cdr. James H. Flatley, Jr.	VF-42, 10	4+	(6.5)
Lt(jg) Walter A. Haas	VF-42, 3	4.83	(6)
Lt. Leslie H. Kerr, Jr.	VF-23	4.83	(6)
Ens. William W. McLachlin	VC-5	4	(5.5)
Lt. Robert S. Merritt	VF-8 (I), 72, 6 (I)	3+	(5)
Lt. Harry A. March, Jr.	VF-6 (I), 17	4+	(5)
Ens. Arthur H. Munson	VF-27	4.5	(5)
Ens. Harry A. Nelson	VF-20	4.16	(5+)
Lt. Robert P. Ross	VF-24	3+	(5.5)
Lt. John F. Sutherland	VF-8 (I), 72, 10	4+	(5)
Ens. Edward G. Wendorf	VF-16	4.5	(5+)
Lt.Cdr. Robert A. Winston	VF-31	4+	(5)

Note: 4+ indicates that "assists" or other uncertain results were recorded at one time, raising total credits to about five.

BOMBER ACES

By long custom and by AFAA definition, only *fighter pilots* qualify as fighter aces. However, two Naval Aviators scored in carrier-based scout bombers (John Leppla and William H. Harris) en route to five credited victories, while Swede Vejtasa's first credits were in SBDs. Additionally, the following Navy patrol-plane commanders had crews with five or more shootdowns in the Pacific Theater, all in PB4Ys.

BOMBER ACES (Cont'd.)

Patrol Plane Commander	Squadron	Score	Primary gunner
Lt(jg) Sheldon L. Sutton	VPB-117	7	
Lt. Paul F. Stevens	VPB-104	6	
Lt. Paul J. Bruneau	VB-115	5	
Lt(jg) Jan B. Carter	VBP-117	5	
Lt. Thomas J. Hyland	VPB-117	5	
Lt.Cdr. H. M. McGaughey	VPB-117	5	
Lt. Daniel E. Moore	VPB-117	5	S1/c R.H. Thomas
Lt.Cdr. Neil C. Porter	VD-3	5	ARM2/c P.A. Ganshirt

Patrol-type aircraft in the Navy and Marine Corps claimed at least 377 aerial victories, including 12 by night-fighter PV-1s. The huge majority of VP claims were by Consolidated PB4Y-1 Liberators and PB4Y-2 Privateers, with 317 of the total.

APPENDIX C

THE SHIPS

The following ships embarked fighter squadrons at some time during WW II. Few escort carriers are listed because CVEs mostly operated composite squadrons (VC) which included both fighters and bombers.

Fast Carriers

Number & Name	*Commissioned*	*Comments*
CV-2 Lexington	14 Dec 27	Sunk 8 May 42
CV-3 Saratoga	16 Nov 27	
CV-4 Ranger	4 Jun 34	
CV-5 Yorktown	30 Oct 37	Sunk 7 Jun 42
CV-6 Enterprise	12 May 38	
CV-7 Wasp	25 Apr 40	Sunk 15 Sep 42
CV-8 Hornet	20 Oct 41	Sunk 26 Oct 42
CV-9 Essex	31 Dec 42	
CV-10 Yorktown II	15 Apr 43	
CV-11 Intrepid	16 Aug 43	
CV-12 Hornet II	29 Nov 43	
CV-13 Franklin	31 Jan 44	
CV-14 Ticonderoga	8 May 44	
CV-15 Randolph	9 Oct 44	
CV-16 Lexington II	17 Feb 43	
CV-17 Bunker Hill	25 May 43	
CV-18 Wasp II	24 Nov 43	
CV-19 Hancock	15 Apr 44	
CV-20 Bennington	6 Aug 44	
CV-21 Boxer	16 Apr 45	
CVL-22 Independence	14 Jan 43	
CVL-23 Princeton	25 Feb 43	Sunk 24 Oct 44
CVL-24 Belleau Wood	31 Mar 43	
CVL-25 Cowpens	28 May 43	
CVL-26 Monterey	17 Jun 43	
CVL-27 Langley	31 Aug 43	
CVL-28 Cabot	24 Jul 43	
CVL-29 Bataan	17 Nov 43	
CVL-30 San Jacinto	15 Dec 43	
CV-31 Bon Homme Richard	26 Nov 44	
CV-38 Shangri-La	15 Sep 44	

Escort Carriers

CVE-16 Nassau	20 Aug 42	
CVE-20 Barnes	20 Feb 43	
CVE-26 Sangamon	25 Aug 42	
CVE-27 Suwanee	24 Sep 42	
CVE-28 Chenango	19 Sep 42	
CVE-29 Santee	24 Aug 42	
CVE-65 Wake Island	7 Nov 43	
CVE-69 Kasaan Bay	4 Dec 43	
CVE-70 Fanshaw Bay	9 Dec 43	
CVE-72 Tulagi	21 Dec 43	
CVE-77 Marcus Island	26 Jan 44	
CVE-108 Kula Gulf	12 May 45	

SELECTED BIOGRAPHIES

The following 12 biographies represent not only the top-scoring Navy aces, but those who made lasting contributions beyond their victory scores, or whose aerial combat achievements were unique. They are listed in order of confirmed victories, with highest wartime rank listed.

COMMANDER DAVID McCAMPBELL (34-5-1)

The top-ranking Navy ace of all time is destined to retain that title. Since 1945 very few naval aviators have even seen 34 enemy aircraft, let alone destroyed that many.

Dave McCampbell was groomed early for a military career. Born in Bessemer, Alabama, 16 January 1910, he attended Staunton Military Academy in Virginia with an Arizonan named Barry Goldwater. McCampbell then spent a year at Georgia Tech before entering the Naval Academy in 1929.

While at Annapolis, McCampbell excelled in diving and won an NCAA regional championship. Upon gradation in 1933, half of McCampbell's class was released from active duty owing to budget restraints. Upon recall a year later, he

Cdr. Dave McCampbell with Leroy Grumman (left) and Jake Swirbul at the famed Grumman "Iron Works."

applied for flight training but was turned down for inadequate vision. However, he persevered and finally won his wings in April 1938.

Assigned to VF-4 on the East Coast, McCampbell soon earned a reputation as a superior gunner. He also enjoyed the social aspects, and a squadronmate once recalled, "Dave and I were asked to leave most of the better restaurants in New York City!"

Lt. McCampbell's first wartime service was as senior landing signal officer aboard *Wasp* (CV-7). He made Navy history during a 1942 ferry run to Malta when an RAF Spitfire lost its drop tank on launch. The Canadian pilot was given a choice: bail out or try to come aboard, and Pilot Officer Jerry Smith elected to try for the deck. McCampbell waved him off the first pass but gave him a premature "cut" on the second. Smith got his wheels on the deck, stood on the brakes, and stopped six paces from the forward edge. That night, McCampbell presented the young Canadian with a pair of naval aviator wings.

McCampbell was still aboard *Wasp* when she was torpedoed by a Japanese submarine off the Solomons in September 1942. Decades later he joked, "I always thought that if my ship was sunk, I'd do a layout and maybe a one-and-a-half gainer. Instead, I looked down, held my nose and jumped in like a kid in a pond!"

Reassigned to the States, McCampbell established VF-15 in September 1943. By the time the air group deployed in *Essex* (CV-9) the following spring, he was a full commander leading "Fabled Fifteen" as CAG, but continued to fly fighters. On his last gunnery flight before leaving for combat, McCampbell shot the tow line in two. He concluded, "I got to the point where I just couldn't get any better."

McCampbell's first victory was a Zeke over saipan on 11 June 1944. To the seasoned old pro, it was anticlimactic: "I knew I could shoot him down, and I did."

On the morning of 19 June, McCampbell's score was two. That afternoon, following the Turkey Shoot, it was nine, as he splashed seven raiders in two sorties.

By 21 October McCampbell passed Alex Vraciu's previous record 19 kills to become the top Navy ace. Three days later he flew the greatest American fighter mission of the war, scrambling from *Essex* with her last seven Hellcats to meet yet another incoming raid. In 90 minutes he claimed nine confirmed and two probables while his wingman, Lt(jg) Roy Rushing, got six confirmed. Dave McCampbell remains the only American fighter pilot to become an ace in a day on two occasions.

At the end of the deployment in November, McCampbell's personal record stood at 34-5-1. Moreover, VF-15 held the record of 310 confirmed kills while the air group had sunk more enemy tonnage than any other such unit in the U.S. Navy. Consequently, McCampbell received the Medal of Honor—the fourth and last carrier aviator so decorated during WW II. He also was awarded the Navy Cross, Silver Star, three DFCs, and the Air Medal.

McCampbell was promoted to captain in 1952 and commanded an oiler before becoming skipper of *Bon Homme Richard* (CVA-31), the only MOH winner to command a carrier. He was still aboard when Wayne Morris, a VF-15 ace, movie star, and nephew by marriage, died of a heart attack in September 1959.

After retirement in 1964, McCampbell tinkered with boating in the Caribbean before settling in Lake Worth, Florida. He liked to tell the story on himself when, circa 1980, he was guest of honor at the P-47 Thunderbolt Pilots' Association meeting. The master of ceremonies said, "Now we come to Dave McCampbell. He's 70 years old; he shot down 34 airplanes; he's been married five times; and he still has more torque than a P-47!"

"Dashing Dave" McCampbell was elected to the Carrier Aviation Hall of Fame in 1981. He died on June 30, 1996.

LIEUTENANT CECIL E. HARRIS (23-1-0)

Like top Marine Corps ace Joe Foss, Cecil Harris rose from South Dakota farm country. He was born in Faulkton on 2 December 1916 and attended North State Teacher's College. While there he enrolled in the Navy's V-5 program in March 1941. Following flight training at NAS Corpus Christi, Texas, Harris was commissioned an ensign on 2 April 1942 and joined Escort Fighting Squadron 27 the next month.

"Cece" Harris' initial combat came aboard *Suwannee* (ACV-27) during Operation Torch, the Allied invasion of North Africa in November 1942. Subsequently the squadron sailed to Guadalcanal, mainly flying from shore March-July 1943. In a roving combat between Cape Esperance and the Russells on 1 April 1943, Fighting 27 claimed six confirmed and two probable Zekes. Lt(jg) Harris got at least one of the confirmed kills. Though he has always been credited with two victories in the Solomons, documentation only exists for one.

Subsequently Harris flew with VC-18 in the Marshall Islands, which became VF-36 (15 August 1943) before redesignation as the second VF-18 (7 March 1944). During workups prior to deployment, he became a pillar of VF-18, admired by the junior pilots for his ability and leadership.

Lt. Cecil Harris (right) discusses the merits of the Hellcat with Cdr. John Raby.

Upon embarking in *Intrepid* (CV-11) in the fall of 1944, now a 27-year-old "bull lieutenant," Harris was a mature fighter pilot. He proved that fact convincingly by destroying eight enemy aircraft in his first two combats, with four kills each on 13 September and 12 October. He added three Judies on the 14th, then supported another pilot in splashing a Betty a week later. It was the only fight in which he failed to claim a kill.

Harris bagged a pair of Pete floatplanes on the 24th, the main day of the Leyte Gulf battle, then destroyed four more fighters on the 29th. He had made 13 kills in 18 days that month.

On 19 November Harris killed a Zeke, tying him with Alex Vraciu as the Navy's second-ranking ace. On the 25th he downed three Tojos in a morning mission to Nielson Field, becoming only the second Navy pilot to surpass 20 victories. He was airborne again during the noon hour, and splashed a Zeke near the ship. However, upon return to the task group, he found "Evil I" had sustained *kamikaze* damage. Cecil Harris' war was over.

Harris scored one-day quadruples on four occasions—a record unique in Navy and Marine Corps history. His decorations included the Navy Cross, two Silver Stars, three DFCs, and three Air Medals.

Remaining in the Navy, Harris completed his education degree in 1946 but was recalled to active duty during the Korean War. Promoted to captain in 1962, he retired in that grade five years later. He remained in the Washington, D.C. area and, in a tragic end to an exceptional life, he died in police custody on his 65th birthday, 2 December 1981.

LIEUTENANT EUGENE A. VALENCIA (23-2-2)

Flamboyant, outgoing Gene Valencia was one of those fighter pilots who loved the game. Younger than Connie Nooy by two days, Valencia became an ace at 22, remaining youngest among all Navy pilots with more than 15 victories.

Hailing from San Francisco, Valencia attended junior college there before entering the Naval Aviation Cadet program in August 1941. He was commissioned a 21-year-old ensign in February 1942 and joined VF-9 a year later. During the *Essex* (CV-9) pcruise of 1943-44, Lt(jg) Valencia claimed 7.5 victories, including three Zekes over Truk Atoll on 17 February. Following that deployment he was widely quoted as saying of the Hellcat, "I love this airplane so much that if it could cook, I'd marry it."

Air Group Nine reformed at NAS Pasco, Washington, where Valencia trained his new division to a very high standard. Sometimes bribing the line crew with liquor for extra gasoline, he molded Jim French, Joe Roquemore, and Clinton Smith into a deadly-efficient team. However, en route to WestPac in late 1944, Roquemore died of pneumonia. A quiet former dive bomber pilot, Harris Mitchell, joined the team as Valencia's wingman.

Twelve months to the day after the Truk raid, Valencia was back in combat—over Japan. He splashed a Tony on 16 February 1945 and added two more kills the 17th.

The next 60 days were active but unproductive for "Valencia's Flying Circus." However, off Okinawa on 17 April the team tied into a flock of bandits and Valencia bagged six Franks, plus one probably destroyed and one damaged. His team accounted for eight more confirmed.

Still hunting near Okinawa on 4 May, Valencia gunned a pair of Vals plus one and a half Franks. He thus became only the third Navy pilot to attain 20 confirmed victories. Valencia's fifth combat of the cruise—and last of his career—

occurred a week later when he claimed three single-engine fighters and a probable.

Valencia's postwar career was richly varied. He served three years as an ordnance officer, two years in an antisubmarine billet, and rounded out his education at the University of California. Next he was assigned to a transport squadron, gaining his third stripe as a commander in 1954.

Valencia's final operational unit was VF(AW)-3, the only Navy squadron in North American Air Defense Command. Flying Douglas F4D-1 Skyrays, the "Blue Nemesis" won the NORAD Achievement Award three years running, 1959-61, the last year under Valencia's command. He retired as a commander on 1 November 1962, holding the Navy Cross, four DFCs, and four Air Medals.

A co-founder of the American Fighter Aces Association, Valencia did more than anyone to establish relations with former enemies in Germany and Japan. He died at the AFAA reunion in San Antonio on 15 September 1972, only age 51. However, he had lived to see the next generation of American fighter aces join the fold.

Lt. Gene Valencia (left) with Leroy Grumman, 1945. He told Grumman, "I'd marry a Hellcat."

LIEUTENANT PATRICK D. FLEMING (19-0-0)

Pat Fleming was an Army brat who became the only ace from the Annapolis class of '41. He was also perhaps the most lethal fighter pilot the Navy ever produced, destroying all 19 airborne targets he engaged.

Lt. Pat Fleming with VF-80 in 1944.

Following a surface tour in cruisers, Fleming applied for flight training and won his wings in 1943. Held over as an instructor, he joined VF-80 in March 1944. His division's section leader was Lt(jg) Zeke Cormier, a former TBF pilot from the Atlantic. Part way through the tour, Fleming became exec of VBF-80, taking his division with him.

Fleming shot down 19 enemy aircraft in six combats between 5 November 1944 and 17 February 1945. His first kill, a Zeke near Manila, was his only single. He bagged four fighters on 14 December, three on 3 January, five on 16 February and four more the next day. On the last two days, he downed nine planes in 20 hours. His division claimed 30+ kills, with Cormier contributing eight.

During a postwar tour at Patuxent River, Fleming's family lived near two other aces: Marion Carl (VMF-223) and Butch Davenport (VF-17), who recalled, "Erin Fleming was the most beautiful child I ever saw." Thirty years later she became Groucho Marx's full-time companion near the end of the comedian's life.

In January 1947, Lt. Cdr. Fleming transferred to the Army Air Force at the invitation of General Curtiss LeMay, who was building the Strategic Air Command. After the Air Force became a separate service later that year, Fleming became a fast-track candidate with an immediate promotion to lieutenant colonel. With his combat and Navy test experience, he joined Colonel Al Boyd's fighter evaluation section at Wright-Patterson AFB. However, his professional future was tied to bombers. In 1952 he joined a B-47 unit, the 306th Medium Bomb Wing, then flew B-29s and B-50s in Japan.

As a full colonel, Fleming became deputy commander of the 93rd Bomb Wing at Castle AFB. Flying as a B-52 instructor, he died in the first Stratofortress crash, 16 February 1956. He was sitting between the pilot and copilot when a generator failed and punctured a fuel tank. Fleming was the only one aboard without an ejection seat, and his parachute caught fire. He bailed out but died on the 11th anniversary of the Tokyo strike when he became an ace in a day. He was 38 years old.

The last word on Pat Fleming belongs to his friend and fellow ace and test pilot, Marion Carl: "Pat was ambitious in a nice sort of way and capable to boot—sometimes a rare combination."

LIEUTENANT (jg) CORNELIUS N. NOOY (19-3-2)

"Connie" Nooy was born in Smithtown, New York, 15 April 1921, and graduated from Long Island High School in 1939. He studied horticulture at New York State Institute of Agriculture, then entered in the Naval Aviation Cadet program in August 1942.

Ensign Nooy won his wings in January 1943 and reported to Lt.Cdr. Bob Winston's VF-31 in April. His first combat from *Cabot* (CVL-28) occurred over Kwajalein on 29 January 1944 when the Meataxers claimed five kills. Nooy was credited with a Zeke confirmed and a probable—the fewest claims he would ever make in one combat.

Now a JG, Nooy was again flying with the skipper on 30 March when the division splashed nine Judies 50 miles from the task force. Nooy got credit for two.

Nooy missed all the action in the Marianas but compensated over Iwo Jima on 4 July. FitRon 31 claimed 13 Zekes that morning, four and a probable going to the squadron's newest ace.

As the fast carriers raided the Philippines, Nooy's star only rose higher. A morning sweep over Negros on 13 September netted him three Oscars and two damaged, raising his tally to ten.

A week later Nooy logged his masterpiece mission. On the 21st—the Meataxers' best day of the war—the squadron notched 29 kills. Thirteen came that afternoon during a strike on Clark Field. Intercepted inbound to the target, the Hellcats engaged enemy army and navy fighters, and Nooy gunned four. Out of ammunition, he then flew a fifth into the ground and proceeded to put his 500-pound bomb into a hangar. It was another Navy Cross performance, raising his score to 15 confirmed and two probables. Fighting 31's second tour, in *Belleau Wood* (CVL-24), resulted in only three more combats. In his only fight of the cruise, 25 July, Nooy bagged four Franks plus a probable—perilously close to becoming only the second two-time ace in a day. Thus, he tied Pat Fleming and Alex Vraciu as the Navy's fourth-ranked ace.

Upon returning to civilian life in December 1945, Nooy held three Navy Crosses, two Silver Stars, two DFCs and six Air Medals. He retained his reserve commission and was promoted to lieutenant commander in 1952.

Lt. (jg) Cornelius Nooy of VF-31.

Entering business in New York, the fighter ace became vice president of American Partition Company. Tragically, Nooy died in Manhattan on 12 March 1958, a victim of cancer while still a young man of 36.

LIEUTENANT ALEXANDER VRACIU (19-0-1)

"Vraciu: rhymes with 'cashew'," Alex likes to explain. The Romanian surname has confused writers for decades, but young Alex spent most of his youth in East Chicago, Indiana, where he was born 2 November 1918. He attended DePauw University, and became semi-famous for a classroom prank by jumping from a second-floor window into a blanket held by some fraternity brothers.

Vraciu gained a pilot's license in 1940 and joined the Navy in June 1941. Designated a naval aviator in August 1942, he reported to Butch O'Hare's VF-3 (soon redesignated VF-6) and was selected as the skipper's wingman. By the time the squadron entered combat from *Independence (CVL-22)*, Vraciu was a junior-grade lieutenant leading the second section in the division. His first victory was a Zeke during the Wake Island strike of 5 October 1943, followed by a Betty on 20 November. A week later *Enterprise* CAG Butch O'Hare disappeared at night near the Gilberts; Vraciu was stunned.

With Fighting Six largely reunited from various CVLs, the squadron supported the Kwajalein invasion in January 1944. On the 29th Vraciu splashed three Bettys in a long, low-level chase, becoming the Navy's 41st ace. Over Truk on 17 February he claimed four fighters, but "Evil I" was torpedoed and steamed to the West Coast for repairs. Vraciu requested to remain in combat.

Reporting aboard VF-16 in *Lexington (CV-16)*, Vraciu found repeated action. He put two Hellcats in the water in five weeks ("I was Grumman's best customer") but became the Navy's fifth double ace on 29 April, during the second Truk raid.

With the opening of the Marianas campaign, Vraciu ran his string to 12 with a Betty near Saipan on 14 June. Five days later he scrambled from Lex to intercept a large Japanese carrier strike, but lagged behind the Airdales owing to a faulty supercharger. Nevertheless, he latched onto a squadron of Judy dive bombers and, in eight minutes, destroyed six. Shooting from close range, he expended only 360 rounds of .50 caliber. The next afternoon, on a strike against

Lt. Alex Vraciu mounts his Hellcat.

Japanese carriers, he scored his 19th victory.

Between tours, Al married Kathryn Horn, then returned to WestPac. He briefly joined VF-19, then leaving *Lexington*, but flew combat with VF-20. However, he was shot down over Luzon on 14 December 1944 (the same day Doug Baker was killed) and led a Filipino guerrilla band. Meanwhile, Kay had the worst month of her life: her father died, her brother was killed in the service, and her husband was missing in action. They were reunited in March.

After the war Al served a tour in Tactical Test at Patuxent River, and spent six years helping establish the Naval Air Reserve. During a nonflying tour aboard *Hornet* (CVA-12) he was selected for commander, and became skipper of VF-51 in 1956. He led the team in the 1957 Navy-Marine aerial gunnery competition with fellow ace Bill Hardy as exec. Flying FJ-4 Furies, the Screaming Eagles placed second in the squadron competition ("the Marines cheated" Al explains) but the skipper won the individual Top Gun spot.

Vraciu retired in 1964 and began a second career with Wells Fargo Bank in the San Francisco area. He was elected President of the American Fighter Aces Association in 1989 and in 1995 was inducted into the Carrier Aviation Hall of Fame with the greatest number of votes yet cast.

LIEUTENANT (jg) DOUGLAS BAKER (16.33-0-1)

Doug Baker lived barely 23 years, but made an enduring record in the last 64 days of his life.

Born in McClain County, Oklahoma, on 27 August 1921, he volunteered for Naval Aviation Cadets on 30 June 1942. Largely owing to the huge backlog, he did not complete flight training until 14 months later, in August 1943.

Ens. Baker joined VF-20 at NAS San Diego in November, five weeks after the squadron was established. Following workups and further training in Hawaii, Air Group 20 boarded *Enterprise* (CV-6) in August 1944. Initial combat involved

Lt. (jg) Doug Baker of VF-20, shown here before his departure for combat.

strikes against the Bonins, Yap, and Palau, but no airborne targets presented themselves through that first line period, ending 21 September.

The squadron's first air combat occurred near Formosa on 11 October. Baker scored the next day, claiming four fighters in a dogfight near Ein Ansho Airfield. During a mission over Manila on the 15th he became VF-20's first ace, adding a pair of Oscars. Six others made ace three days later, 18 October, when he added 3.5 more kills. The the young Oklahoman kept maximizing his opportunities, scoring a solo victory and two shared on 13 November with another Oscar the next day.

Air Group 20 transferred to *Lexington (CV-16)* on 23 November, by which time Baker's 12.33 kills established him as the squadron's top shooter. In fact, he remained the top-scoring ensign in Navy history, as he was promoted to "jaygee" in November.

Doug Baker's last combat remains something of a mystery. On 14 December 1944 he was involved in a combat over Clark Field. He was seen to shoot down three Zekes and an Oscar, then disappeared. His short-term squadronmate, Alex Vraciu, was shot down by flak that day and eventually received Baker's dogtags from Filipino guerillas.

Baker's decorations included two Silver Stars, four DFCs, and eight Air Medals. In 1994 he was honored by induction into the Oklahoma Aviation Hall of Fame as one of his native state's 30 fighter aces.

LIEUTENANT (jg) IRA C. KEPFORD (16-1-1)

The Navy's top land-based fighter pilot, Ike Kepford was also the service's leading Corsair ace.

Born in Harvey, Illinois, on 29 May 1919, Kepford was an outstanding athlete before the war. He played football in high school, and as a quarterback at

Lt. (jg) Ike Kepford in his VF-17 Corsair.

Northwestern University he won all-conference and All-American honors.

Kepford left college in his senior year and entered the Navy in August 1941. Eight months later he began flight training at NAS Glenview, Illinois. Following commissioning as an ensign, he joined Lt.Cdr. Tom Blackburn's VF-17 in January 1943 and began mastering the F4U-1 Corsair.

The Jolly Rogers were prevented from sailing to combat with the rest of Air Group 17 when *Bunker Hill* (CV-17) was unable to provide enough F4U spare parts. Therefore, Blackburn's Irregulars went to the northern Solomon Islands in October.

Ens. Kepford made an auspicious combat debut in support of the U.S. carrier raid on Rabaul, New Britain, 11 November. Stretching his fuel to the limit, he claimed three Vals and a Kate destroyed plus one Val damaged.

Newly promoted to JG, Kepford became the Navy's third Corsair ace on 27 January 1944 (after Tom Blackburn and Clement Gile) and the service's first F4U double ace thereafter. He was the first-ever Navy pilot to 15 kills and, at the end of VF-17's tour in March 1944, he led the entire Navy with 16 victories. He had been awarded two Navy Crosses, a Silver Star, and the DFC.

With Lt.Cdr. Rog Hedrick and several other VF-17 veterans, Kepford helped form VF-84 in May 1944. However, Kepford was detached from the Wolf Gang in December and spent the remainder of the war in the States. He left active duty in November 1945 but retained his reserve commission, eventually attaining lieutenant commander.

After the Navy, Kepford entered business and became a regional president of Liggett-Rexall Drug Company. He died in Harbor Springs, Michigan, 19 January 1987, at the age of 67.

Lt. (jg) Charlie Stimpson in his VF-11 Wildcat at Guadalcanal, 1943

LIEUTENANT CHARLES R. STIMPSON (16-2-0)

Tall, skinny, almost cadaverous, the cheerful, extroverted "Skull" Stimpson was very much a people person—and one of the finest fighter pilots of his generation.

Born in Salt Lake on 24 August 1919, Charlie Stimpson grew up in Santa Barbara, California, and attended Pomona College. After graduation in 1941 he was accepted for Navy flight training, which he completed in June 1942. In August, Stimpson went to NAS North Island, San Diego, where the gangly ensign joined the newly-estabished VF-11. The Sundowners were one of the last F4F-4 squadrons, arriving for a land-based tour at Guadalcanal in April 1943. By then Stimpson was a "jaygee" leading a four-plane division.

In three months at "Cactus" Stimpson had only three combats, beginng 16 June. On that occasion, intercepting large Japanese formations, he latched onto a batch of Vals and expertly destroyed four in his first fight. Three weeks later, on 6 July, he became an ace by downing a Zeke, with his sixth kill—another Zeke—recorded three days later. When the Sundowners left The Canal later that month, Charlie was the top scorer.

After reforming at Alameda with F6Fs and further training in Hawaii, VF-11 finally got to the carrier war aboard *Hornet* (CV-12) in September 1944. Charlie retained his place as the Sundowners' top shooter by destroying ten planes in three missions. Lt. Stimpson's first combat of the deployment occurred off Formosa 14 October when he claimed three Hamps and two Zekes destroyed with two Tonys as probables. Thus, he not only became an ace in a day, but one of four pilots to make ace in both F4Fs and F6Fs.

During strikes over the Philippines on 5 November, Stimpson bagged two Oscars and a Tojo. In his sixth and last combat of the war, 14 November, he downed a Tony and a Zeke. Discounting two "singles," he destroyed 14 planes in just four missions.

Stimpson finished his wartime service at NAS Corpus Christi, then transferred to the inactive reserve.

Settling in Southern California, Charlie married into the hotel business. He spent the last several years of his life as the genial, popular host of The Inn at Rancho Santa Fe. Few of his guests had any idea of his combat record, though one of them once asked, "Weren't you scared?" Leaning back in his chair in the elegant dining room, Charlie quipped, "Gosh, I'm scared right now!"

Charlie Stimpson died 20 August 1983, four days short of his 64th birthday. Appropriately, he was attending a Blue Angels performance at NAS Miramar. He was one of the *nicest* men the author has ever known.

LIEUTENANT COMMANDER EDWARD H. O'HARE (7-1-0)

Known as Butch at the Naval Academy, O'Hare was always "Eddie" to his family in St. Louis. His father, also Eddie, was a Chicago attorney who ran afoul of the Al Capone gang and was murdered in 1938.

After graduation from Annapolis in the Class of '37, O'Hare served two years aboard USS *New Mexico*. Exposed to naval aviation as observer in the battleship's floatplanes, he entered Pensacola in June 1939 and emerged with his wings of gold 12 months later. Sent to Fighting Three at San Diego, he soon established a solid reputation as an aviator and especially as an aerial marksman. He developed into one of Lt.Cdr. Jimmy Thach's most adept pupils.

O'Hare won national fame for his defense of *Lexington* (CV-2) on 20 February 1942. Following a canceled strike on the Japanese naval-air complex at

Rabaul, New Britain, VF-3 scrambled 18 Wildcats to defend against an equal number of Mitsubishi G4M bombers. In the action, Thach's pilots destroyed 13 but the second prong of the attack approached from the disengaged side.

O'Hare was up with his wingman, Ens. Marion Dufilho, whose guns jammed. But undaunted, Butch attacked alone. In three firing passes he shot five bombers out of formation, and landed aboard low on fuel and ammo. His first request was for a glass of water.

In all, Fighting Three splashed 15 bombers against two F4Fs and one pilot lost. O'Hare actually destroyed three and badly damaged one, with lesser damage to another. Hailed as the first Navy ace of the war, he was returned to the States, where he received a two-grade promotion to lieutenant commander. President Roosevelt presented O'Hare the Medal of Honor on 21 April 1942.

Now a lieutenant commander, O'Hare assumed command of VF-3 in mid-June, eventually returning with the squadron to San Diego. However, by the next summer he was back in Hawaii, where the outfit was redesignated VF-6 in July 1943. O'Hare worked his pilots hard that spring and summer. The squadron re-quipped with F6F-3s and set about learning its new weapons, though some pilots cadged flights in Army P-40s, somewhat to the CO's displeasure. However, for a period O'Hare "owned" an F4U-1 Corsair, which he obviously relished.

Fighting Six was deployed in several light carriers in time for the opening of the Central Pacific Offensive. O'Hare's detachment boarded *Independence* (CVL-22) for the Wake Island strike of 5 October, and he demonstrated that he had lost none of his touch in the 20 months since Rabaul. In that mission—only his second combat—O'Hare became a genuine ace by destroying a Zeke and a Betty. His section leader was a new jaygee named Alex Vraciu, who opened his own account on 5 October.

Lt. Cdr. Butch O'Hare, Medal of Honor.

By then O'Hare had been promoted to command Air Group Six, and shortly he moved to *Enterprise*. There his FitRon briefly was the new VF-2 while the Felixes regrouped. Meanwhile, Cdr. Bill Dean's Rippers had experimented with "bat teams" of two F6F-3s working with radar-equipped TBF-1Cs. The experiment was tried for real during the Tarawa invasion of November 1943.

On the night of the 26th, O'Hare with Ens. Andy Skon as his wingman launched from the Big E with Lt.Cdr. John Phillips of VT-6. Some 15 Betty torpedo planes harassed the task group, and Phillips was vectored onto two bombers, which he shot down. Calling for a rendezvous, the torpedo skipper orbited while the two fighters tried to join up. From that point, accounts vary, but apparently the Americans' RV point was within visual distance of the enemy aircraft. O'Hare's F6F got between the Avenger and at least one Betty, and tracer fire erupted in both directions. Skon had the briefest glimpse of his CAG slumped forward in the cockpit, then lost sight. Butch O'Hare was dead at age 29.

Nominated for a second Medal of Honor, O'Hare was posthumously awarded a Navy Cross in addition to two DFCs. A destroyer (DD-889) was named for him, as was Chicago's major airport. The O'Hare family's authorized biography by Dr. Steve Ewing and John B. Lundstrom was published in 1997.

COMMANDER JOHN S. THACH (6-1-0)

John Smith Thach was named for his brother James—at least that's how the midshipmen at Annapolis explained it, if not his family in Pine Bluff, Arkansas. The elder brother graduated in the Class of '23, and the family resemblance was so strong that upper classmen who saw the new kid dubbed him accordingly. Thus was born the legend of Jimmy Thach.

Ensign Thach left the Naval Academy in 1927 and began the requisite surface duty before becoming eligible for flight training. Leaving the battleship *California*, Thach reported to Pensacola in March 1929 and was designated an aviator ten months later. He reported to VF-1 in early 1930, and when he departed in July 1932, seven years would pass before he returned to fighters.

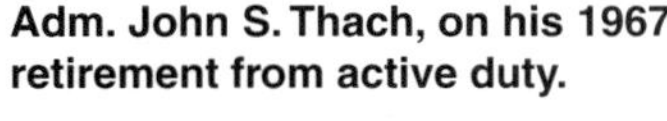

Adm. John S. Thach, on his 1967 retirement from active duty.

Some indication of Thach's early talent is evident in the fact that, as a junior aviator, he became a test pilot at NAB Hampton Roads, Virginia, barely two years out of flight training. His subsequent squadron assignments were in patrol and observation units, but he made notable contributions. In 1935, while in PatRon Nine, he flew the Hall XP2H-1 from Norfolk, Virginia, to the Panama Canal Zone. At the time the seaplane was the largest aircraft built in the United States.

In June 1939 Lt. Thach was ordered to Fighting Three at San Diego. It was a meeting of the man and the moment. As gunnery officer, Thach was free to develop his theories on aerial gunnery. As a long-time pheasant hunter, he already knew about deflection shooting. As for tactics, he and other pilots maneuvered matchboxes around his kitchen table in Coronado, leading to the "beam defense" technique which eventually bore his name.

At the time of Pearl Harbor Thach was CO VF-3, promoted to lieutenant commander on New Year's Day 1942. As part of *Saratoga* Air Group, Fighting Three was orphaned when "Sara" was torpedoed 11 January. However, after relieving VF-2 in *Lexington (CV-2)*, Thach took his F4F-3s into combat during the abortive strike on Rabaul, New Britain, on 20 January. In the same action in which garnered Butch O'Hare a Medal of Honor, Thach's pilots splashed 15 of 18 G4M1 Bettys, losing one pilot and two Wildcats. The CO was involved in three shootdowns that day, sharing a patrol plane in the morning while adding a Betty and half of another in the afternoon.

Three and a half months passed before Thach again fired his guns in earnest. With just ten VF-3 pilots (including eight rookies) he moved aboard *Yorktown (CV-5)*, absorbing 16 VF-42 veterans from the Coral Sea action. Hastily repaired, *Yorktown* departed Pearl Harbor 27 May with Thach's F4F-4s—destination Midway.

On the morning of 4 June Thach led five other Wildcats to escort *Yorktown's* SBDs and TBDs against the Japanese carriers northwest of Midway. In the first combat test of the Thach Weave, VF-3 claimed six kills against one loss, with the skipper splashing three. Though his "beam defense" was proven conclusively, Thach's tiny formation was swarmed by perhaps 20 Zeros, preventing direct support of Torpedo Three, which was destroyed.

That afternoon, though *Yorktown* had been damaged in a Japanese attack, Thach led a wild scramble to intercept *Hiryu's* torpedo squadron. The skipper splashed one Nakajima B5N2 and probably another, then recovered aboard *Hornet (CV-8)*. *Yorktown* was severely damaged, never to recover, and Thach inherited a diverse, shaky command. Fighting Eight was leaderless but Thach quickly melded the various elements into "VF-3/42/8" for the rest of the battle.

Following Midway, Thach served two years in Training Command at NAS Jacksonville, Florida, then joined the staff of the Fast Carrier Task Force. As an operations officer for Vice Adms. Marc Mitscher and John McCain, he remained in WestPac until the formal surrender in Tokyo Bay in September 1945. As a captain he returned to Jacksonville until the start of the Korean War, when he commanded the escort carrier *Sicily* for more than a year. Subsequently he commanded the second *Midway*, *Franklin D. Roosevelt*, and was promoted to rear admiral in 1955.

Much of Thach's work as a flag officer involved antisubmarine operations, further enhancing his reputation for versatility. He was "Op-05," the deputy chief of naval operations for air warfare, from 1963 to 1965, and retired with four stars in 1967. While still on active duty he was elected fourth president of the American Fighter Aces Association.

Admiral James S. Thach (Ret.) died 15 April 1981, four days short of his 76th birthday.

AVIATION PILOT FIRST CLASS LEE P. MANKIN, JR. (5-1-3)

The only enlisted ace in Navy history, Paul Mankin also became the youngest Navy officer to retire as a captain.

Born in Mammoth Springs, Arkansas, 26 October 1920, Mankin enlisted in the Navy at age 17. After completing electronics school, and still a teenager, he became a radioman aboard the battleship *California* before transferring to aviation. He served in VP-22 and VB-3 before qualifying for noncommissioned flight training. As a Naval Aviation Pilot he pinned on his wings of gold on 9 February 1942 and reported to VF-2, "The Flying Chiefs," the next month. Three months later Mankin transferred to Fighting Six in *Enterprise (CV-6)*.

Aviation Pilot 1st Class Mankin was airborne in an F4F-4 on 7 August 1942, supporting the Guadalcanal landings. Shortly past mid-day, Fighting Six intercepted 27 Mitsubishi G4Ms of the Fourth Naval Air Group from Rabaul, intent on sinking the U.S. transports.

In Lt(jg) Gordon Firebaugh's division, Mankin was unable to drop his belly tank but pressed the fight regardless. Making high-side passes at the Bettys, he flamed one before a Zero jumped his section leader, Ens. Bob Disque. Mankin could not quite cut the corner to pull lead on the Zero, but his tracers forced the Japanese to disengage. Perilously low on fuel, he ignored *Enterprise's* red flag and landed from a port turn. His engine died of fuel exhaustion seconds later.

During the Eastern Solomons carrier battle of 24 August, Mankin flew with Ens. George Brooks' division. Defending the Big E from carrier-based air attack, VF-6 fought a widespread, confusing battle. Red Six division was first vectored far to the northwest before it was obvious that the Japanese formations had eluded detection. When Brooks' pilots found targets, it was an odd mixture of enemy bombers and *Saratoga* SBDs in a bizarre tailchase. In the confusing intercept, Mankin claimed two Aichis destroyed, including one which burned.

Lee Mankin, ace of VF-6 and VF-5, shown here as a lieutenant commander. He retired a captain.

However, *Enterprise* had sustained bomb damage, and many of her pilots landed aboard "Sara." Among the 16 fighter pilots retained and absorbed into Fighting Five were six NAPs, including Mankin. With 3-0-1, he was a valuable addition to Roy Simpler's outfit.

"Sara's" spaciousness was a short-lived luxury for the newcomers. On 11 September, VF-5 staged up to Guadalcanal to join the Cactus Air Force, badly in need of the Navy's 24 Wildcats and pilots. Paul Mankin landed just behind the skipper, being designated Simpler's wingman. The squadron was in combat the next day.

Scrambled to intercept bombers, Mankin nursed a Wildcat with a sluggish engine. Attacking alone, he gunned a Betty but got "sucked" astern, vulnerable to return fire. The enemy tail gunner shot up the F4F, putting a 20mm fragment into Mankin's boot, but one bomber succumbed.

Late that month Mankin fought a three-day mini campaign. In a close-range fight the 27th, he destroyed a Zero to become a 21-year-old ace. The next day he damaged two bombers and, in a frightening one-v-four, he claimed a Zero probable the 29th.

That was the end of Mankin's air combat, though he flew escort and antishipping attacks thereafter. He departed Guadalcanal on 14 October, eventually receiving two DFCs and an Air Medal.

Upon return to the States, Mankin was commissioned in January 1943 and reassigned to the Atlantic Fleet. There he joined VC-55 in the escort carrier *Block Island* (CVE-21), sunk by a U-boat in May 1944. After being detached from VC-55 he became a landing signal officer on the new carrier *Midway* (CVB-41).

Lt. Mankin attended Stanford University from 1948 to 1950, then returned to flight status. In a change of pace for a carrier aviator and LSO, he flew with Transport Squadron Five from 1950 to 1952, then returned to shipboard duty in tender *Salisbury Sound* (AV-13) for a year. During that tour he was promoted to lieutenant commander, attaining commander four years later.

Upon retiring from the Navy in 1958, Paul Mankin was advanced to captain on the basis of combat decorations. At age 37, he was the youngest officer to attain that rank. Subsequently he retired to Whidbey Island, Washington, devoting much of his time to fishing.

RECOMMENDED READING

American Fighter Aces Assn. *American Fighter Aces Album.* Mesa, AZ, 1996.

Bruce, Roy W. and Charles R. Leonard. *Crommelin's Thunderbirds: Air Group 12 Strikes the Heart of Japan.* Naval Institute Press, Annapolis, 1994.

Hammell, Eric. *Aces Against Japan.* Presidio Press, Novato, CA, 1992.

Hata, I. and Izawa, Y., translated by D.C. Gorham. *Japanese Naval Aces and Fighter Units in WW II.* Naval Institute Press, Annapolis, 1989.

Jensen, Oliver. *Carrier War.* Simon and Schuster, New York, 1945.

Lambert, John W. *Wildcats Over Casablanca: Operation Torch.* Phalanx, St. Paul, 1992.

Lundstrom, John B. *The First Team: Naval Air Combat from Pearl Harbor to Midway.* Naval Institute Press, Annapolis, 1984.

—— *The First Team and the Guadalcanal Campaign.* Naval Institute Press, Annapolis, 1994.

Mersky, Peter. *The Grim Reapers: Fighting Squadron Ten in WW II.* Champlin Museum Press, Mesa, AZ, 1986.

Olynyk, Frank. *USN Credits for Destruction of Enemy Aircraft.* Privately published, Aurora, Ohio, 1982.

—— *Stars and Bars: A Tribute to the American Fighter Ace.* Grub Street, UK, 1995.

Reynolds, Clark G. *The Fighting Lady.* Pictorial Histories, Missoula, 1985. (*Yorktown*, CV-10)

Sims, Edward H. *Greatest Fighter Missions.* Harper Brothers, New York, 1962.

Stafford, Edward P. *The Big E.* Dell, New York, 1964. (*Enterprise*, CV-6)

Tillman, Barrett. *Carrier Battle in the Philippine Sea.* Phalanx, St. Paul, 1994.

—— *Sundowners: VF-11 in WW II.* Phalanx, St. Paul, 1993.

—— *Corsair: the F4U in WW II and Korea.* Naval Institute Press, Annapolis, 1979.

—— *Hellcat: the F6F in WW II.* Naval Institute Press, Annapolis, 1979.

—— *Wildcat: the F4F in WW II.* Naval Institute Press, Annapolis, 1989.

—— *Hellcats: A Novel of the War in the Pacific.* Brassey's, McLean, VA, 1996.

MEMOIRS BY WW II NAVY FIGHTER PILOTS

when known

Blackburn, Tom. *The Jolly Rogers.* Orion Books, New York, 1985. (VF-17)

Cormier, Richard L. (with Wally Schirra, Phil Wood, and Barrett Tillman). *Wildcats to Tomcats: The Tailhook Navy.* Phalanx, St. Paul, MN, 1995. (VF/VBF-80)

Erickson, Roy D. *Tail End Charlies.* Privately published, Pasadena, CA, 1995. (VBF-10)

Galvin, John R. *Salvation for a Doomed Zoomie.* Allnut Publishing, Indian Hills, CO, 1983. (VF-8)

Smith, John F. *Hellcats Over the Philippine Deep.* Sunflower Manhattan, KA 1995

Winston, Robert A. *Fighting Squadron.* Holiday House, New York, 1946. (VF-31)

Winters, T. Hugh. *Skipper: Confessions of a Fighter Squadron Commander.* CFM Press, Mesa, AZ, 1984. (VF-19)

Wordell, M.T., and Seiler, E.N. *Wildcats Over Casablanca.* Little, Brown & Co., New York, 1943. (VF-41)

Also see the novels of Jack Newhafer (VF-5 and -6), especially *The Last Tally-Ho* and *No More Bugles.*

Index